HOW TO SAVE YOUR OWN LIFE

MICHAEL GATES GILL

GOTHAM
BOOKS

HOW
TO SAVE
YOUR OWN
LIFE

15 Lessons on
Finding Hope in
Unexpected Places

GOTHAM BOOKS
Published by Penguin Group (USA) Inc.
375 Hudson Street, New York, New York 10014, U.S.A.

Penguin Group (Canada), 90 Eglinton Avenue East, Suite 700, Toronto, Ontario M4P 2Y3, Canada
(a division of Pearson Penguin Canada Inc.); Penguin Books Ltd, 80 Strand, London WC2R 0RL,
England; Penguin Ireland, 25 St Stephen's Green, Dublin 2, Ireland (a division of Penguin Books
Ltd); Penguin Group (Australia), 250 Camberwell Road, Camberwell, Victoria 3124, Australia (a di-
vision of Pearson Australia Group Pty Ltd); Penguin Books India Pvt Ltd, 11 Community Centre,
Panchsheel Park, New Delhi—110 017, India; Penguin Group (NZ), 67 Apollo Drive, Rosedale,
North Shore 0632, New Zealand (a division of Pearson New Zealand Ltd); Penguin Books (South
Africa) (Pty) Ltd, 24 Sturdee Avenue, Rosebank, Johannesburg 2196, South Africa

Penguin Books Ltd, Registered Offices: 80 Strand, London WC2R 0RL, England

Published by Gotham Books, a member of Penguin Group (USA) Inc.

First printing, December 2009
10 9 8 7 6 5 4 3 2 1

Gotham Books and the skyscraper logo are trademarks of Penguin Group (USA) Inc.

LIBRARY OF CONGRESS CATALOGING-IN-PUBLICATION DATA

Gill, Michael (Michael Gates)
How to save your own life : 15 lessons on finding hope in unexpected
places / by Michael Gates Gill.
p. cm.
ISBN 978-1-59240-521-3 (hardcover)
1. Happiness. 2. Hope. 3. Life skills. 4. Gill, Michael (Michale Gates) I. Title.
BF575.H27G555 2009
158—dc22   2009028093

ISBN 978-1-592-40521-3

Printed in the United States of America
Set in Apollo MT

Penguin is committed to publishing works of quality and integrity.
In that spirit, we are proud to offer this book to our readers;
however, the story, the experiences, and the words
are the author's alone.

This book is dedicated to Alison Larkin,
a true friend and a great writer.

CONTENTS

INTRODUCTION

BLESSINGS IN DISGUISE

When I was fired from my job and then diagnosed with a brain tumor, I thought my life was over.

And I was right.

My old life was over.

But then a whole new and better life began.

What I did not expect was that I could create a new life that would make me happier than ever. While no one would ever voluntarily choose personal or professional disasters, such shocking experiences can be blessings in disguise.

Sometimes, when the things we fear the most happen, loss can surprise us and give us a chance to find a whole new level of happiness.

For it is not what life brings to you but what you bring to life that can make all the difference.

In the following pages you will find true-life lessons that will help you cope with the inevitable misfortunes of our world that may hit you, often when you least expect it. These lessons will also help you create a life you love.

By following these 15 simple lessons—"the 15 L's," I call them—you will be able to make the hard times into some of the best times of your life.

These lessons have been hard-won. I would not voluntarily have set out to learn any of them. Yet life grabbed me by the neck and threw me out of my privileged spot at the top of the American Establishment. It was only through this expulsion that I was able to learn.

I was born the favored son of a famous father. Brendan Gill worked for *The New Yorker* magazine. This was before the Internet had become so pervasive and before television had become a vehicle for twenty-four-hour news and drama. In my father's era print was a dominant medium, and his magazine was regarded as the greatest literary source of contemporary insight and distinguished writing in America. Every week people would look forward to a new story by J. D. Salinger, or follow a piece of Truman Capote's new "nonfiction" realism with horrified fascination, or laugh at James Thurber's madcap illustrations and his original humor.

My father brought home many of these illustrious writers and artists to play with me in our twenty-five-room mansion. E. B. White, author of *Charlotte's Web* and *Stuart Little*, would bend to tell me that he always thought it was "such a shame to grow up." Charles Addams, whose cartoons were the inspiration for *The Addams Family* on television, would stand in a corner wearing a helmet from the Middle Ages to get me to laugh.

Later in life Ernest Hemingway would challenge me to run before the bulls in Pamplona (an offer I barely survived).

I went to fancy parties with Jackie Onassis and other glitterati of the world when it seemed like these intelligent, attractive people could accomplish anything.

I was given a Yale education—admittedly because my family had gone there for generations.

After Yale, a Yale Man who owned the largest advertising agency in the world gave me a job.

every wish was met. And they were: I was given a gymnasium to play in and a Steinway grand piano to play on when I was a child. I followed my father to Yale and into the powerful secret society of Skull & Bones. I received an inheritance from my grandfather that allowed me to travel and see the world. My job was given to me because of my Yale connections. Having been given everything, I was completely unprepared to lose anything.

That was why I was so shocked when, at fifty-three, I watched my American Dream turn into my worst nightmare.

I was invited out to breakfast and fired.

I had defined myself through my job as a creative director and executive vice president of J. Walter Thompson. I had never been given a bad performance review, but I realized too late I had made an unforgivable career mistake: growing old in advertising. I was devastated to have my reason for being—my sense of self—taken away.

I literally burst into tears after I heard the fateful news.

Yet I could not tell anybody the truth of what I was feeling. If you complain of bad treatment in corporate America, it is like breaking the oath of silence in the Mafia—you will experience a quick death in your profession—you will never be hired again.

So I didn't complain about being fired. I even pretended to my family and friends that I was happy to have a chance to go out on my own.

I just couldn't admit even to myself what a fool I had been to trust my fate to a corporation. In some sense, I had given my life to them. I worked long hours; I traveled to meetings without any notice. I missed my precious children's recitals and chances to spend leisure time with my family. I toiled away to do my job perfectly and to please my clients and the company heads. But I learned the hard way. Just because I was loyal to them for twenty-six years and went everywhere they asked and did everything they asked of me, it didn't mean they would be loyal to me. Profits were more important than people.

After being "let go," I tried to run an independent consulting firm but quickly discovered the horrifying silence at the other end of the phone when you have reached a certain age and are still trying to sell yourself as someone with great, fresh advertising ideas. Feeling less and less confident, I looked for self-affirmation outside my marriage and that led to having an affair and a divorce. I had always thought of myself as a great family man and yet I realized I had betrayed the trust of my wife and the children I loved.

I couldn't understand what was happening to me but I felt helpless to do anything except what I already knew how to do. In a sick form of wishful thinking I still dressed up in my Brooks Brothers suit every day and acted like an advertising big shot. When in truth I was becoming poorer and poorer and feeling worse and worse.

I knew I was failing but did not know how to change it.

Finally, at sixty-three I went for a "routine" physical and was diagnosed with an acoustic neuroma—a noncancerous but potentially dangerous brain tumor. I had no health insurance by that time—having let the corporate contract lapse—so my doctor agreed to postpone the operation.

Full of remorse for the mistakes I'd made and living in a black cloud of despair, I went back to visit the neighborhood on the Upper East Side of Manhattan where I had spent my earliest years as a fortunate son. I felt like my life was over and I was desperate for a warm reminder of the favored place in the universe I had occupied when I was growing up.

That neighborhood had been my kingdom. Even the police officers would sometimes salute me on the street and give me a badge to wear for a few moments.

Now I seemed to have become invisible to everyone.

I noticed a new Starbucks store on the corner. I went in to have what I was thinking might be my last latte . . . like a condemned man treating himself to a last meal.

Inside, there was a young African-American woman—a store manager—who was hoping to hire somebody that day. She offered me a job. With a desperate kind of courage I said yes.

It was an opportunity that would change my life in so many ways.

Fortunately, I was able to record this transformation as it happened day by day. My daughter Annie had suggested when I was having so many hard times that I keep a journal as a way of helping life settle. I would write a sentence or two before I went to sleep at night. After about a year of working at Starbucks I reread the journal. I read my descriptions of how despairing and depressed and fearful I was at the beginning, and then, just a year later, how happy I had become. Happier than I had ever been in my life.

This was a huge shock to me. Why was I happier now in what many would think was a menial job serving other people coffee than I had ever been in my high-status job manipulating people at JWT?

Maybe that very sentence provides an important clue. Instead of spending my day convincing people to do things I wanted them to do as I had in my previous advertising life, as a Starbucks barista I was focused on serving others in exactly the way they wanted.

I had been told in my Starbucks training that there was only one answer to any Guest request: an enthusiastic "Yes!"

I had come to see that there was a kind of joy in serving others that was not possible when you were trying to control others.

Another source of happiness was my new humility. I had come

to realize that I was not a Master of the Universe but rather another particle of energy in the ever-expanding universe.

My life today is so different from my former world. I have to be in to "open" my store at 5 A.M., but by noon I can leave, having completed my shift. I have worked hard to serve coffee, take out the garbage, and do the hundreds of other small yet vital tasks that allow customers an enjoyable experience in the store.

Then—the rest of the day is mine.

I remember an occasion in my previous life in advertising when I got a call from my boss on Christmas Day. My children were just beginning to unwrap their presents. I was told that it was an emergency—we had to shoot a commercial immediately to get it on the Super Bowl.

I left my young family without a thought.

That is how mixed-up my priorities were.

I never stopped thinking about ads and office politics. I worked twelve-hour days and traveled several hundred thousand miles a year. I had little time for my children, my friends, or even my own life.

Today, as I walk out the door of my store, I own my own life again.

Last week I followed my shift at Starbucks with meeting my daughter Annie for a birthday lunch. It sounds so crazy to me now but to be honest, in my old advertising life, I might have decided I was too busy even to make time for a birthday lunch with my daughter.

As a creative director I spent many hours handling what were regarded as "emergencies." A client might be unhappy with an ad. That was an emergency. A talented art director might decide to turn over his desk in frustration, endangering storyboards we had already sold to a client. I would have to run down the hall to calm things down and make sure that the storyboards were safe—

even if the art director was upset. It was like being a doctor on call in an emergency room except that I wasn't saving lives—I was catering to outsize egos and selling ads.

Looking back I have to admit that I was so obsessed with my job, I had bought into the idea that everything that happened was a life and death matter.

I cannot believe today how much of those thousands of hours of mine were spent in meetings. Just as depicted in the television series *Mad Men* (and we were basically all men and all mad in our focus on our jobs rather than our families), we would go into meetings first thing, with coffee and cigarettes, and end the day in a place actually called "The Meeting," which was an in-house bar that JWT maintained at the top of the Graybar Building.

All of our meetings were regarded as vital. Reports were written and circulated. Meetings were regarded as such an important part of our lives that if you missed a meeting or—even worse—were not invited to a meeting, you were worried that you might be on your way out the door.

Today we have no such meaningless meetings at my Starbucks store. We are too busy serving others to spend time talking to ourselves.

Which has given me more time to spend with my children.

I recently went down to Washington, D.C., to spend a couple of days with my daughter Laura, who was also having a birthday celebration.

I also took a weekend to travel up to Boston to be with my son Charles on his birthday.

In other words, I have time for my family now and recognize how precious that time is. I don't regard my children's birthdays as obligations to be squeezed into my busy days, but rather as precious blessings to be fully enjoyed.

My new happiness at Starbucks flowed from its gift of a part-time job that gave me a full-time life.

Before, my life was full of advertising problems, and even when I was at home I would be thinking of office politics and the next meeting. New-business meetings. Meetings about meetings that had happened and new "crucial" meetings to come.

Many of the meetings were about how to reach our "target groups," usually young, affluent high achievers between twenty-five and thirty-five. If we could get them to buy our cars or toothpaste or vitamins, others would follow.

We spent many hours analyzing the demographics and psychographics. We learned to judge people by what they wore rather than who they were.

With the help of Crystal, my first store manager at Starbucks, I learned that such superficial judgments were not necessary or encouraged or even allowed anymore.

I still recall the day I learned the importance of not judging people solely by appearances.

A homeless man entered our store. I had just finished cleaning the bathroom. Full of newfound pride in my ability to make it sparkle like a Ferrari, I stepped in front of him. I could see he was heading right for the bathroom and wasn't going to have one of our fancy lattes.

"The bathroom is out of order," I told him.

The homeless man turned without a word and left. He was used to such rejections. New York City has few public restrooms, and homeless people often try and fail to use the facilities of bars and restaurants.

He was not surprised. I was relieved that my clean bathroom could remain pristine.

But Crystal came over to me. I could see she was upset.

"Don't ever do that again," she told me. "Just as I respect you, so should you respect others. Everyone who comes into our store is a welcome Guest. Everyone deserves to use our facilities. The last thing that gentleman needed today was to be disrespected by you."

Crystal helped me see the new radical truth: I could not be worthy of her respect if I did not respect others. And that I had to learn to respect people not because of the way they looked or who they were, but *because* they were. That each human being, whatever their circumstances, deserved respect.

Today, with the help of my Partners on each shift, I am able to understand that each individual—on both sides of the counter—is worthy of respect.

Another reason I am so happy today is that I have found in the simple life of serving and living without stuff a whole new life I had never imagined.

The act of serving someone a good cup of coffee is so much more satisfying and enjoyable than sitting in a meeting trying to figure out how to manipulate someone into buying something they might not need.

I cannot tell you how much more fun it is to share a laugh or a story with someone in a coffee bar rather than trying to persuade a client to buy a multimillion-dollar ad campaign.

I am so much happier wearing a green apron and moving fast to serve others than I ever was in my Brooks Brothers suit, trapped in another meeting to discuss whether someone at Ford thought a Mustang commercial we shot was "too western."

Helping people—my Partners and my Guests—even in the smallest ways, to enjoy each day is so much more uplifting than worrying about the well-being of overpaid CEOs.

After working for a year at Starbucks, when I read back over the journal my daughter Annie had suggested I keep, I was amazed at how much happier I had become once I had left behind those external measures of success.

When I was going through hard times, I looked for books to help me and found none. I love to read and look to books for inspiration and information. But most of the books in bookstores and libraries were about how to make a fortune on Wall Street or get rich in real estate. I wasn't able to find a single book about how to go from riches to rags in America—and still find an even more fulfilling life.

There was no book that told the story of how, without having all the high-status stuff, you could find a new sense of happiness. So I thought my story was something others who were facing hard times would like to hear.

I wrote it all out and titled it *How Starbucks Saved My Life*.

It became a *New York Times* bestseller.

I would like to think that my book became so popular because it had the sparkling prose of F. Scott Fitzgerald or the vivid scenes of contemporary life described with the flair and wit of Jane Austen. But I have to admit my book was a hit because it struck a powerful chord in the lives of people who were struggling with new challenges every day. It was a story they needed to hear, and it helped them to move forward.

During my book tours I have had a chance to speak with literally thousands of people. I *have* heard that my story has been helpful to many who have been fired, or lost their homes, or even to those who have been diagnosed with serious diseases and have no health insurance.

My story is about stumbling and losing in life, but it delivers the good news that there is life—even a better life—after losing the external measures of success. The people I talk with seem reassured and even inspired by my surprising story of the joys of finding my new, simpler life. It took me nearly sixty-five years, and I had to learn the hardest way possible, but eventually, I was able to save my own life. And I've never felt happier, more fulfilled, and more engaged. It is my hope that people don't have to make the same mistakes I did before they learn to live fully.

That is why I have now written this book for *you*. *If someone like me found a way to save his own life, surely others can do the same.*

That is why I've called this book *How to Save Your Own Life*.

In the next few pages you will read concrete lessons and examples of specific actions you can take to make your life better and more fulfilling—today.

I have found that hearing my story helps others, and I hope sharing these new life lessons will help you too.

HOW TO SAVE YOUR OWN LIFE

Listen . . . To Others Who Have Suffered and Survived

"A problem shared is a problem halved."
—*English Proverb*

 The other day I was standing in line at the checkout counter of a grocery store when a man came up to me, clearly upset and shaking with anxiety.

"I read your book," he said. "I recognize you from TV."

I nodded. It was my local store and he was my neighbor, so I smiled—not just to indicate that I welcomed his presence but also to calm him down.

Not only was he literally shaking, but his hair was wild and uncombed, and he looked like he had not shaved for days. "I need to speak to you," he said. "I am near the edge. You talked of thinking at one time *you* were near the end."

"Yes," I said as the line inched forward. "How can I help?"

"No one can really help," he said, twisting his face almost into a snarl. It seemed full of anger—as much against the world as against me.

"What happened?" I stammered, hoping to keep him talking

as he hugged the grocery bag he was carrying and looked toward the exit.

He was about to leave. He turned.

I sensed that he was embarrassed even to be there, in a public place, asking for anyone's help. His instinct when he had recognized me, as a guy who had made it through some hard times, had been powerful, though.

He had reached out to me. I sensed he knew he'd involuntarily cried for help.

But now as he glanced around with red-rimmed eyes, I could tell he was hoping to escape and forget that this encounter had ever happened.

Yet he leaned a little closer to me, as though to confide a secret.

"I worked for years," he said, "like you. But I had my own business. I built it up *myself*!"

Here I heard a clear ring of pride in his voice. Compared to me, he had really achieved something. I had only received a high-profile job through my connections. A Skull & Bones friend had offered me a job in the largest advertising agency in the world, and I'd ridden to my corporate life on the back of my birth and legacy and social position.

My neighbor's tone seemed to imply—which was his right and was also probably accurate—that in my corporate life as a top advertising executive, I had merely been a comfortable passenger on a huge train. Starting a company yourself took pride and courage that merely working for a company did not.

"But recently," he continued, his voice taking on a kind of complaining, rasping sound, "with these greedy bankers . . ."

He left the sentence incomplete.

The line was moving. I stepped forward. He now followed me.

"I've been screwed," he said. "The business I built over a life-time is . . ."

He couldn't bring out the words.

"I'm broke. The business is done."

Tears actually started into his eyes.

I could sympathize. When I was fired, I stepped out into the street and wept. I knew how frightening it was to feel threatened in your professional life—especially if you defined yourself by that life, as I once had. Having experienced the shocking loss of a job myself, I was able to sympathize with his situation. In the past I might have thought: "It's your own fault."

But now I have come to a more humble and true view of the world: Oftentimes life can be like a car accident when you are hit by a drunk driver. It is not your fault; you just happened to be in the wrong place at the wrong time. I think it is wise for all of us to remember that injunction: "There but for the grace of God go I."

So I listened to my new friend with real sympathy—I had, in my own life, been in some measure where he was that day.

"I have a big house up the hill," he said, gesturing so forcibly that he almost hit a lady trying to get by. He jumped back.

"Sorry, sorry," he said, truly concerned that he had almost hit her. I could sense that underneath the stress he was a kind man, but at this moment he had reached a point where he was out of control. His life was a mess, his hair was wild, and he couldn't even seem to control his limbs.

"I am going to lose my house," he continued.

I stepped out of the line. I guided him to a quiet corner by the produce section.

"What am I going to do?" he did not so much ask me as him-self in a kind of anguished mutter under his breath.

"My kids love it here. It's the only home they've known. If I lose my house and we leave here . . ." He saw the future, and it was terrible to him.

"It's all over for me," he said too loudly. "And for them," he stated more sadly and softly. I listened intently, trying to recall the same sensation that I know I had felt many years back; it had been more than ten years since I had lost my job.

He continued. "My son George is eleven and my daughter Alice is just five. They will never forgive me for this."

"I dedicated my book to my kids," I said, "for their understanding hearts."

He stared off into space. He clearly wasn't listening.

In this moment he didn't care what I had or had not done. "I'm thinking of ending it all," he said and seemed to get ready to leave. He was turning away.

"Look," I said urgently, "I don't think your kids care if you are broke. They'd like to have their dad around."

But he was leaving now. I called out in a loud voice at his retreating back, "Don't you think your kids would miss you?"

I wasn't going to let him get away.

I remembered at that instant a terrible time in the past when I had done nothing to stop a man who was also shaking with anxiety and clearly on a downward path.

I was working late to prepare for a major Ford presentation. I was in my early thirties and had just been promoted to a position as a creative director. I knew that I was going to be tested and I wanted to be prepared, since Ford liked to do what they called "beating up on the agency."

I was working hard to make sure I had all the ads done just right when Bob North came into my office.

I knew Bob was in trouble.

He was an account guy. Bob was very intelligent but very shy. He had a hard time expressing his opinions. Ford likes them big and tough and I had seen the Ford client demolish him in meetings. Bob was also—in my eyes—too old for his job. He was forty. His blond hair was turning gray. I thought Bob should be the boss of his own account by now—with a title as vice president and account manager at least—not simply another lowly suit, one of many scrambling to survive on the high-pressure Ford business.

I was surprised to see him late that night in my office. Creative people didn't spend much time talking to "suits." It was not a welcome intrusion. I was so busy and so anxious to prepare a good presentation, I didn't want any interruptions—especially from a suit.

"Mike," Bob said, "do you have a minute?"

I looked up, tired and stressed. Before me I saw a man who seemed full of anxiety. It felt like a disease I didn't want to catch. His fear and weakness could be contagious—or at the very least a major distraction—and I still had a lot of work to do.

"Actually, no, I don't have time," I said, a comment I today regard as terrible cruelty. "But what's on your mind?"

Bob took a tentative step or two into my office. He seemed so bowed down by the world. He was six feet two—Ford liked account guys to be tall. But Bob was way too thin. And now he was hunched over, his shoulders collapsing into his skinny chest.

"I just want to bounce a few ideas off you," he said in a voice that was soft and shaky.

"About what?"

"I've got a new strategy idea for Mustang."

"Bob," I said with force, now angry and defensive, getting ready to punch back at any such suit intrusion, "I don't have time for this!"

I had just created a whole campaign based on a strategy Bob and the account team had given me weeks ago. My team and I had created many ads for that strategy. I didn't want to change just days away from a major presentation.

"Well," Bob said, his hands shaking as he tried to hold a bunch of strategy papers together, "I just thought maybe we could brainstorm together and come up with something different."

Looking back now on that sad night, I understand that Bob was just trying to find another human being to talk with. He had needed a break from his own anxieties. I realize now that he was just using the new strategy as an excuse to try to spend some time with me because he thought I might be sympathetic to him—not just because he was a suit but because he was a fellow human being who was suffering.

Bob was wrong about me that night.

That night I had no place in my heart for sympathy.

I knew that Bob was not having much luck at Ford. I was sure the rest of his account team had dismissed his ideas. Now he was so desperate he had come to me—a relatively young and open creative guy.

But his request to "brainstorm" that night was the very last thing I wanted to do.

"Something different?" I said, and I didn't disguise my exasperation. "We've got the presentation on Monday. This is Thursday night. You're nuts!" I turned back to my desk, hoping Bob would leave.

"I know," he said, still desperate to connect. "It's just that I was thinking maybe we could position Mustang more as a value car rather than just a sporty car."

"Bob, you're crazy," I literally shouted at him, shocked that he would even think of such a huge departure from what we had planned. "Mustang is fun. Value is boring."

Bob gave up on me and retreated down the hall.

Stressed out myself, I had taken offense at his intrusion rather than seeing him as a human being who was—for whatever reasons—really in pain.

That Saturday I was working in the office with the creative team (in those days I worked most weekends). My boss came down to the creative floor. This was unusual. He usually preferred to stay in his office and have us come to him.

"Mike," he said, "get your team together. We'll meet in the creative conference room."

I thought for a moment that there was going to be some change in the date of the Ford presentation.

"What's up?" I said, still anxious to get back to work. The rest of my team was standing—no one wanted to sit down with so many layouts to design and ads to write before Monday.

"I just want you all to know because you worked with him: Bob North committed suicide last night."

"What?" I stammered stupidly.

I had to sit down.

"Why?" someone asked.

"His wife says he hasn't been feeling well for months."

"Feeling well?" I said.

"Bob's wife used the word 'stress,'" my boss said quietly. "It's a real tragedy.

"But I just don't know what she means by 'stress,'" my boss continued with more strength in his voice.

He looked around the room.

"We're *all* stressed out," he said, almost angry now. "But we don't commit suicide. Days before one of the most important presentations. We'll find out more," he concluded. "In the meantime, let's get back to work!"

And that's exactly what we did. And *I* never bothered to find out more about what happened to Bob.

Now, looking back, I can see I was probably just one more person who didn't give Bob what he needed to stop him from taking his life. I was just as stressed as Bob was and unable to see beyond my own self-concern to reach out to a man who needed help.

I remembered at that moment someone who had listened to me when I needed help.

Kevin Buckley had been a friend from my wild Yale days. I remember once knocking a bottle of champagne off the bar in my eagerness for another glass of bubbly. The heavy champagne bottle happened to land on Kevin's foot.

Kevin lived in my dormitory, and as I passed his door late the next day—I always got up late at Yale—I saw his foot bandaged and raised above his bed.

"Kevin?"

"Yes, Gates."

"Me?"

"Yes. Broke my toe."

I stepped into his room. "I am so sorry."

"It is nothing. Being stuck here will help force me to get my work done."

Kevin *did* get his work done. Unlike me, he had worked hard to get into Yale. Unlike me, he was not rich. Unlike me, he didn't treat Yale as a chance to party.

In addition to his academic work, Kevin also worked hard and became a reporter and later managing editor of the *Yale Daily News*—which was one of the most challenging jobs on campus.

After college Kevin went almost immediately to the top of his profession: He became *Newsweek*'s bureau chief in Vietnam during the era of star reporters like David Halberstam.

Afterward, he also worked in London and New York as a reporter and editor. He had been awarded a Nieman Fellowship at Harvard, the greatest honor in journalism.

Kevin and I remained friends after Yale, and when I was having my hard times, Kevin happened to call me up just to see what I was doing. We agreed to have lunch.

Kevin told me he was writing and teaching at Columbia.

At first I was embarrassed to tell Kevin how far I had fallen from the golden youth he had known. Yet in his sympathetic presence, I decided to trust him and tell him the truth: that I was virtually broke, struggling to find work, had fathered a child outside my marriage and was divorced, and had recently been diagnosed with a brain tumor.

Kevin had known me when I had been a rich and profligate undergraduate, blessed with a fortunate life that seemed like it would continue forever.

His face filled with sympathy as he heard of my struggles.

He listened for hours as I told him the truth of all I had been through.

After lunch Kevin gave me a hug, and he promised to stay in touch and try to help, and I knew that he was being sincere.

Sometimes you can sense that someone really cares just by their listening. I knew Kevin really cared about me—that he was still devoted to our friendship born in such wild circumstances so many years ago.

I realized an important truth: Despite all that had happened to change my life, Kevin was still my friend. And just having a chance to tell him—to tell someone—the truth about what I was going through was a huge relief.

I had tried before to share my desperate condition and feelings of failure with another old friend from Yale. We had drinks at his club. He left me on the pavement afterward with a quick wave of his hand, and I had the distinct sense that he never wanted to hear from me again.

For that old "friend" it was almost as though my financial and personal failures could be catchy—like some kind of social disease.

In fact, that's the way I felt myself, so I didn't blame him. I kept the secret of my failures to myself and told myself that it was best to present a brave face to the world—even to the world of old friends.

Kevin was different. He didn't disappear after I opened up and shared my struggles with him.

Kevin tried to help by finding me some advertising work. He called on his contacts from the publishing world to try to get me some introductions. He was not successful. Once again, I think I was just too old to be the person someone wanted to hire to create the next bubble gum campaign.

But Kevin tried, and just his effort made me grateful. He would also call me up at least once a week just to check in. He wrote me e-mails, which he signed "With love."

Kevin showed by word and deed that he was not about to abandon me although my circumstances had changed so dramatically. He listened to me, and just by listening so patiently and sympathetically, he helped me get through a time when I had lost my confidence.

I vowed at that moment in the grocery store that I would be more like Kevin. I would not let another human being—also shaking with anxiety, also so clearly in need of someone to hear his problems—get away.

I was not going to be too busy or too polite to help this man. I *shouted* at him again to remember his children: "Wouldn't your kids miss you?" I called out loudly at his retreating back.

He stopped.

I could see him giving that idea some thought—probably for the first time. He turned to face me.

"Yes," he said, "I guess my kids *would* miss me. They don't even like it when I am away for a couple of days on a business trip."

"One mistake I made," I said, "was I didn't talk to my kids when I messed up my life."

"Talk? What can I tell them? Your dad screwed up and we have to leave the place where you grew up?"

"What I found," I explained, "was that my kids were a lot wiser about life than I was. They also appreciated it when I leveled with them about what I had done. How's your relationship with your wife?"

"My wife is fine. She says everything will be okay and that she loves me blah blah blah."

"Blah blah blah?"

"Doris doesn't get it. I told her we were broke and had to move and that I'd have to start over at the bottom"—here he glanced at me—"just like you. But she just said she loved me and we'd make it. She has no sense of reality."

"Look," I said, realizing I had said more than enough already. "Before you do anything too drastic, just go home and talk with your kids."

"But they are just kids," he said.

"That's the point," I said.

"Okay." The last word he more or less threw at me over his shoulder. He was not a happy man as he headed out of the grocery store that day.

Several days after our run-in at the grocery store, he entered the Starbucks store where I have worked as a barista for the last five years. He didn't even order a drink. He was coming to find me.

I was busy taking out the garbage. He stopped me as I got outside. I almost didn't recognize him. He had shaved. His hair was combed.

"Thanks," he said, giving me a little hug even though I was carrying a bag full of soggy coffee grinds. I staggered a bit as he put his arm around me.

"Sorry," he said. "I just wanted to stop by and to see you before I go. I've got to leave Bronxville. I can't afford the mortgage on my house anymore. But I'm *not* going to leave my life—or my family!"

"Good," I said.

"And my kids reacted great," he said. "Just like you predicted. My kids regard the whole thing—the move and everything—as a great adventure."

He shook his head, smiling.

Readers of my book often come in to see me, enjoy a latte, and tell me their stories. I've also heard from many more through mail, e-mail, and phone.

I've been overwhelmed by how much my personal story has struck a chord with people throughout the world.

Many people have told me of how they've been inspired by my story and how I reversed the American Dream—"tragically" going from riches to rags only to discover, much to my surprise, that I was happier than I had ever been.

My story has helped them find a life they love.

The other day a twenty-eight-year-old woman came into my store and told me: "Your book so inspired me that I quit a job that was boring me to death, and I am now doing something I really love."

She explained to me that she had taken a job in an investment bank straight out of college. It was profitable, but it dead-ended her. Now she found herself much happier and more fulfilled working at a nonprofit helping teach inner-city kids.

I am so grateful and honored that the story of my life—full of my own painful struggles—has inspired others like her to save their own lives.

You can learn a lot about yourself by listening to someone else's struggles. Often, someone else's mistakes, and the lessons they learned as a result, allow you to avoid making the same mistakes yourself—and allow you to absorb the critical life lessons learned and use them to guide you to a better life.

When I was a young, arrogant executive—thinking I was immune to problems—I was never able to listen to others' problems seriously. Until I found myself one day with bigger problems than I could ever imagine. Until then, I didn't know how important it was to listen to others. Take the time to hear their troubles and to understand what they have gone through.

Just as I listened to my neighbor in the grocery store, my neighbor had listened to my problems through reading my book and had been able to reach out to me.

And this woman, much younger than I was, had read my book and had drawn the lessons from the story of my mistakes. She had been open to understanding someone else's experiences, and she had allowed them to inform her own opinions. Without realizing it, I had helped her change her own life.

In such a way she had learned a life lesson in her twenties that I had only discovered when I was in my sixth decade.

HOW THIS LESSON CAN HELP YOU

Too often in America we automatically answer the question: "How are you?" with an automatic: "Fine!"

But this is often not truthful—especially in these challenging times.

You can learn to be more open and willing to tell someone when you are in pain. Often someone else will share an experience that can help you make it through even the worst kind of tragedy.

A tragedy shared becomes less of a trauma and more of a way to experience a new and deeper emotion that can lead to a better way to live.

By sharing your problems with others who have encountered true suffering and survived, you will be able to move forward in a more positive way. And simply by taking the time to listen to the problems of others, you will help ease someone else's burdens.

Listen . . . To Your Own Heart
to Find True Happiness

"I will arise and go now, and go to Innisfree, . . .
And I shall have some peace there, . . . for always
night and day I hear lake water lapping with low sounds
by the shore; While I stand on the roadway, or on the
pavements gray, I hear it in the deep heart's core."

   —William Butler Yeats, "The Lake Isle of Innisfree"

 I was over sixty years old before I knew what it meant to find peace in my own heart.

Late one night, after closing my Starbucks store on the Upper West Side in Manhattan, I walked out into the rare silence of a city asleep.

I looked up at the sky full of stars that seemed to gleam with a special brilliance. It was a cold winter night. I stopped absolutely still in my tracks before I rushed off to catch a subway. I touched my heart. Only then did I discover how happy I was.

At the risk of missing my train back to Bronxville, I had to walk around the block. I was so shocked. Could I really be so happy? Having just finished mopping up a floor after working at a "low-status" job serving coffee to others?

I had thought I could only be happy in a corner office being served by others.

Once I had led a life where it was taken for granted that I could go on fancy vacations and have a summer home and a small fleet of cars for my family.

How could this new life, this life of doing manual tasks, of serving drinks to others, make me feel anything but depressed?

I came back to the same spot, touched my heart again and realized that, yes, this amazing fact was true; I was now happier than I had ever been before. I had grown up in a cacophonous culture of wealth: a rich, well-connected family and high-powered friends always full of high-sounding expectations. I had created some of the many thousands of noisy ads for big corporations from Ford to Kodak—encouraging a perpetual belief in external measures of success: big cars, bigger houses. I had helped define the American "pursuit of happiness" as an aggressive race to obtain more and more expensive, high-status toys. I thought that life was the right life—until I was fired.

During all my striving and spending I had never really paused to listen to my *own* heart.

There was a "sign-in" pad in the New York office. I loved to be the first one to sign in—before seven A.M. Sometimes Lou Falippo, a guy who worked in the financial area, would beat me in. I hated that! I would leave after seven at night—one of the last of the creative guys to go. I loved to work weekends—when the clients weren't calling, you could get so much more work done. My life was at my office. I checked everything else at the door. And I never even thought of listening to my heart to see if all this striving and business was making me happy.

Now my heart told me that I did not need all those commercial trappings of success.

I didn't need to live in a house anything like the twenty-five-room mansion in which I had grown up.

I thought about all of this as the train sped me back to my new apartment in Bronxville. As I looked out my window I thought of all the other people leading such different lives in so many different circumstances.

In my previous life on such a train I would have been buried in a newspaper. I would read the news compulsively—as though staying up with the latest story was a matter of life and death. I would buy two or three newspapers in the morning: *The New York Times, The Wall Street Journal.* In the evening I would pick up a copy of the *New York Post* and maybe a news magazine. Without realizing it I had become emotionally as well as mentally involved in the news of the day, although I had virtually nothing to do with it and could affect it in no way.

Wars and rumors of wars could upset me, yet leave me powerless to do anything about it. First thing in the morning I filled my mind with all the negative news from around the world, and the same toxic bits of information would be fed into my brain last thing in the evening. My head would be swirling with worries.

Now, this evening, instead of devouring the latest news, I let my heart expand as the train moved past all the different lives being lived in all those various homes.

The home I was heading for tonight was the smallest of my life. I had grown up in big houses. I had always assumed I needed that kind of space to be happy. Yet now I was traveling home and a smile lit up my face. What a relief!

I had struggled so hard through all the years to keep up the big houses and buy more stuff to fill them up. Tonight I felt free from that burden.

Across the aisle I saw a man I knew. Jeremy Tompkins. A lawyer in a big firm. We had been at Yale around the same time. We had been casual friends, nodding to each other as we crossed paths on campus. I had heard from other classmates that Jeremy had become a legal specialist in saving major corporations from paying any taxes. So he had beaten that cliché that nothing is certain but death and taxes. Yet he didn't look like he could beat death—even with his brilliant legal mind.

I thought with sympathy and some concern that he looked very old and tired that night. His shoulders were hunched over. There were strands of white hair on his pin-striped suit. His face was pale and colorless. His hair—what was left of it—was white. Jeremy was in the winter of his days. He had probably earned thousands of dollars in fees that day. Did he look back on the seasons of his life with any real joy?

I saw him adjust the glasses on his thin nose as he perused the distinctive pink pages of the *Financial Times*.

I knew he was going home to a big house. I could see him walking up from the station in my mind's eye. My heart went out to him. In Jeremy I could see much of my former self. A self that took what I had been given for granted. I did not envy him. I guessed that Jeremy probably thought he was relatively happy in his life. I am sure he wanted to believe that he had achieved a great deal. I recalled that his father had been a lawyer in a big firm, too, so Jeremy was marching down the same well-worn track.

I hadn't seen Jeremy in years, yet I knew that if he wrote in to the *Yale Alumni Magazine* and tried to sum up his life, he would not speak of his big house or his workaholic job. He would speak of his new grandchildren. He would talk of a chance meeting with an old friend.

In other words, Jeremy had probably lived most of his life with his head but he would talk about what really mattered to him from his heart. And the fact of the matter, as I learned so late in life, is that the heart doesn't care about how many hours you billed or how much you paid for your home.

The heart doesn't let you lie about what is really important in life.

If Jeremy were honest when he recounted the happiest times of his life he would remember the special times he shared with loved ones. It would not have mattered whether it had been by a campfire in the middle of the woods or on a chance encounter in New York City. Those times of shared happiness would stand out in his mind more than all his material success.

I knew it.

For such had happened to me.

Once I let go of all my headstrong concerns with success, I discovered a whole new life by following my heart.

You can't miss what is truly important in life if you are in touch with your heart.

I knew that Jeremy was not an evil person or even a bad man. But in my eyes that night, his was a life filled with busywork—just like mine had been—that neither he nor anyone else would remember.

Every civilization needs people like Jeremy and lawyers and bankers, and advertising guys like I had been. But to spend life with your head totally locked away from your heart cannot be healthy for anyone.

I suddenly thought back to 1990 and the words of a minister in a Fifth Avenue church. Joseph Straight's sermons were sometimes a little hard to take. He could dissect every word in the Bible with a kind of intellectual force that took away some of the magic and a lot of the emotion. Like pinning down butterflies.

He spoke to me of those who were about to die.

"It was quite a shock to me, at first," Joseph told me. "These old guys who had built up huge fortunes on Wall Street, who had spent their passion and energy fighting for every dollar. At the end they want to talk about someone they loved. Their wife. One man's dying words were about a girl he had seen only once at the opera but still couldn't get her out of his mind. Others spoke of their children or grandchildren. They all talked about people they loved and who loved them. Not a single big shot mentioned to me anything about his work."

"Why not?" I asked.

Joseph was really an intellectual and a scholar more than a preacher. You know the type. I could see he had given this whole question a lot of thought.

"I believe as these big businessmen near their end they see clearly—maybe for the first time—what really matters in life."

"And that is?" I wanted to hear him say it again.

"Love," Joseph said, although a little embarrassed by the word.

At the time I was talking with Reverend Straight, I would have been embarrassed to speak of love or of listening to your heart as the surest guide to finding happiness. I didn't really hear his words or believe at that time that they applied to me.

Today I understand completely the reason Jesus, when He was asked what were the most important commandments, replied simply: "Love your neighbor as yourself. And love your God with all your heart and soul and mind."

Now I try to love my neighbor as best I can. In a small way I do this each time I serve someone coffee or smile at someone on the street.

I have found that love is not a limited natural resource like gas or oil. In fact, the more you open your heart, the more it seems to fill up with love.

I love God with a constant feeling of gratitude for all the miracles He has given me.

I start the day by repeating a phrase found in the Bible: "This is the day the Lord has made. Rejoice and be glad in it."

Rejoice.

To me that is further proof that we are created to find lives we can love and experience true joy in living.

Love to me no longer simply means "falling in love."

Although I hasten to add that I do not in any way demean the act of falling in love.

I wouldn't be here if my parents had not fallen in love.

When my father first saw my mother when he was visiting his college roommate in the country, he said: "I am going to marry that woman."

It was love at first sight, and I would not have been born unless my father had followed his heart with such confidence. In fact, my grandparents were also a passionate love match. My grandmother fell in love with my grandfather when he grabbed the bridle of her horse after a train had scared it. She claimed later, "Frank saved my life." My grandfather always said, "On the contrary, Madelaine saved my life." They fell in love at first meeting and brought the child into the world who brought *me* into this world. So I am deeply grateful that such powerful passions happen.

Yet I am rather concerned that every song and every movie seems to have as its subject "falling in love," and virtually no songs or movies are about *falling in love with the life you live.*

You can *fall in love with your life.*

So late in life I have fallen in love with the life I have now created. I think sometimes we get glimmers of a life we could fall in love with at a very early age. The key is to be attuned to it, to be aware of what makes you—in your heart—truly happy.

I remember when at ten I fell in love with words—reading and writing and speaking became a kind of passion for me.

Mrs. Farlie, my sixth-grade teacher, would encourage me to read my stories aloud. One character I had created was a rabbit—always getting into trouble at school.

I remember vividly how much fun it was to stand up and read before the class and hear the laughter of my friends clustered around.

Now at sixty-eight, I find myself doing exactly the same thing—and loving the same kind of life: writing and speaking, and even singing.

The poet Wallace Stevens said: "Words of the world are the life of the world."

The Bible says: "In the beginning was the word."

I fell in love with a life full to overflowing with words.

Maybe that is why I stayed so long in advertising. It was a form of using words. But I can truthfully say I didn't love what I did. Twisting words to manipulate was so different from using words to educate or even entertain. I liked the money, but I was never very enthusiastic about the actual business of turning and twisting words to get people to buy things they probably didn't really need.

Yet I spent twenty-six years doing something I didn't really love.

I hope anyone who reads this book will stop now if they are spending their lives in a job they don't truly love and say: "Enough!"

If you don't love what you are doing, do not give your life away by continuing to do it!

How do you find a life you love?

Follow your heart.

By following my heart I have created a whole new life I really love.

I don't mean that it is easy to follow your heart.

When you are young there will be many voices, from parents to well-meaning friends, who might tell you that what you love to do is not "practical." Later in life these voices will stay with you—filling your mind with all the reasons to stay with a job you hate rather than one you really love.

That is a sad fate.

A friend of mine, Dick Rhinebloom, got tired of the advertising business. He went to law school. He became a divorce lawyer. I happened to run into him a few years later.

"How are you doing?" I asked him.

"Terrible," he said.

"What do you mean? Are you sick?"

"No, not physically sick. Just sick of this business. It turns out being a divorce lawyer is even worse than being an advertising guy!"

We laughed, but I realized Dick wasn't kidding. He had stopped doing one thing he hated and had found another profession he hated even more.

"Everyone is so angry every day," Dick continued. "At least in advertising we could fake happiness."

We both laughed again. We had faked it—for ourselves and for the consumers we always pictured laughing happily around the kitchen table at home or happily washing their new Ford.

"So what are you going to do?" I asked.

"Nothing," Dick said. He shook his head with disgust at himself. "The money is too good to quit. I've built up a business. See you in twenty years—in Prague!"

Dick headed off to catch a train. We had always talked of getting to Prague together someday. We had both heard that it was one of the most beautiful cities in Europe.

Dick is probably still working away at a job he hates. It is the money trap. You think you can't get out. And it isn't easy.

If you had twenty lives to live maybe one could be spent piling up the gold—then you could spend it in the next.

But this is it. Your life is the only one you have.

Don't let your head lead you down a "rational" road that can destroy your soul and make you wake up like me after doing something you didn't really love for twenty-six years.

All those years of my life I was not passionately, fully engaged. I was a passenger in life. Not leading my own life.

That night I climbed the stairs to my little attic apartment with a new sense of peace. I loved coming home to this little place. My dining room table was just a plastic picnic table with white plastic chairs. Total cost: $53.00. On the table was a book I was reading given to me by my daughter Elizabeth (whom I call "Bis"). It was called *A New Earth* written by Eckhart Tolle—which I never would have had time to read in my former life. By the side of my bed was my trusty journal. I still try to write a sentence or two every night. There was also a Bible and the Book of Common Prayer.

In the kitchen sat a French press and a teakettle.

Each morning I greeted my day with a great cup of coffee and each afternoon I made myself a cup of strong tea.

As I looked around the little space, I realized with surprise how happy I was in that small, simple apartment.

It had everything I needed.

I walked to the window. Outside I could see a large pine tree, its branches dark against the darker sky.

I think of my little apartment as a kind of tree house. I love being so near the tops of trees and so much a part of the sky.

My heart told me that night and every moment of every day that I don't need those big material comforts I once thought I could not live without. And this doesn't just pertain to material trappings but also to societal decorum. And what a burden has been lifted now that I don't have to worry about high societal expectations anymore.

The other day I got an invitation to a fancy party in New York City. A lot of famous celebrities would be there. I walked over to my white plastic kitchen garbage container ($7.50) and gently dropped the invitation in. I smiled.

While I did not disrespect these people—and I would RSVP politely no, I had other plans—what a relief it was to decide *not* to go to such a big and glamorous party!

I have learned there is new life that can flourish when you set some social limits.

I hasten to add that I still have great affection for all my old friends. It is just that at this stage of my life, if I were going to spend time with anyone, I would prefer it was one of my children. My old friends are not so nurturing to me or necessary to me as they once were.

They haven't changed. But I have. I can no longer stand conversation about the good old days.

To heck with the old days!

Instead of making idle chatter about the state of mutual funds in our IRAs, that night I planned to listen to a symphony and let the images of the day play through my mind.

Since I have left my former life I have learned that true happiness for me is found in small, everyday experiences, not as part of a large crowd. Things I never had time to notice or experience before, things I wasn't paying enough attention to, suddenly offered me a portfolio of rich experiences I'd never be able to get, even if I had become the wealthiest, most successful man in the world. I've been surprised to find gemlike discoveries in the smallest things and sometimes in the most usual experiences and—when you pause to appreciate them—they become the most wonderful. The other day I made a list of a few of the places where I've found unexpected joy:

- In the surprising satisfaction of working really hard to clean a toilet and making a bathroom sparkle like a new car
- In the song I happen to overhear that sends me singing out loud as I walk down the block
- In the warm sun of an early April day that catches me by surprise when I have spent so many months getting used to the cold gray days of winter
- In the delight of going to bed on a rainy afternoon with a good book
- In the deep enjoyment of spending time with my children—simple lunches in the city or long walks in the country—as I observe and marvel as they create their own remarkable lives
- In the feeling of gratitude in waking at the beautiful first light of dawn
- In the simple act of sharing a smile or a joke as I serve others a good cup of coffee
- In walking home in the soft blue dusk of summer and seeing a full moon rising in the sky

In my former life I might have dismissed many of these daily events as too mundane to notice or overlooked them in my anxiety to get on with what I thought was success.

Yet I know now that in my rush I was missing the essence of life that is found for me in the simplest things.

I have discovered so late in life that trusting your own heart is your greatest—and only—path to real happiness.

Listening to what really matters (and accepting what you can control and what you cannot) makes all the difference.

I can't have any influence on whether the stock market or the real estate market goes up or down. I recognize that I can't even be in complete control of whether my brain tumor will grow or whether my barista job will be secure tomorrow in this erratic economy.

I am simply and humbly one more part of this mysterious and amazing and ever-changing universe.

While I can't control all these major external forces, I *can* take control of what affects me so deeply. I can listen to my heart and respond to its needs.

I can be aware of popular measures of success and accept the external buffetings of life *without buying into everyone else's negative or fearful view of the world*.

My life is mine to feel. My life is mine to love.

Being in touch with your heart rather than trying to follow your head is the true guide to a happy life.

When I was working so hard in advertising, I was affronted by a sermon in church one Sunday. The minister preached about "Take no thought to tomorrow." He went on to read that famous passage in the Bible that says:

And why take ye thought for raiment? Consider the lilies of the field, how they grow; they toil not, neither do they spin: yet Solomon in all his glory is not arrayed as one of these. If God so clothed the lily of the fields how much more will he do for thee, o ye of little faith!

On Monday, despite being incredibly busy with about eight new campaigns to create, I called the minister and told him forcefully that I had a problem with his sermon that Sunday.

"I have a wife and kids to clothe. I can't take no thought for tomorrow," I said through clenched teeth.

"Relax, Michael," he told me, hearing my tense, even angry, tone. "That is one of the toughest passages in the Bible for high-achieving Americans to get their heads around."

"Yeah, because it doesn't make sense."

He was losing me.

"How about this?" the minister asked. "How about we see beyond the metaphor for what God might mean?"

"Okay," I said reluctantly, glancing at my watch. I had a meeting with my creative team scheduled in five minutes.

They would be wandering into my office.

I didn't want them to overhear me talking about God—that would not instill confidence.

"You know the passage: 'Take no thought for the morrow.' Do you know what follows?"

"No."

"Just a line or so later we are told: 'Seek you first after the kingdom of God and all these things shall be added unto you.'"

"So?" I was being rude.

But I had a lot of things to do.

I was a busy guy.

Church for me was just one more thing—and not the most important thing—in my life.

The minister continued: "Take that advice: 'Seek you first after the kingdom of God and all these things will be added unto you.' That means you don't have to give up buying clothes for your kids, but just make sure you focus a little more on God rather than giving up every second of your life to mammon."

"Okay. I guess I get it."

He hung up.

I hung up.

But at that time I *hadn't* really gotten it.

I was focused more on my role as I saw myself: a moneymaker, wanting more "mammon" to buy more fancy clothes for my kids and for myself.

Only now do I really understand what the minister was trying to tell me.

We *all* need material items like clothes. But buying clothes should not fill up every inch of our heart and mind and spirit. Such necessary garments should not be how we determine our happiness.

That at least is what I have come to understand today.

I think what the minister was getting at is that such material concerns will always play a role in our lives, but they should not *dominate* our lives or control our feelings.

We should not live and work so hard simply to buy fancy "raiment."

Ralph Waldo Emerson said: "A man is what he thinks about all day."

I was filling my head with advertising junk. I was busy creating ads that were chewing gum for people's eyes. I had no time or even the inclination to consult my own heart.

I believe now that following our hearts is the only way to find true happiness.

Let your heart guide you in how you fill your days . . . like the wind fills the sails of a boat.

Today I pause in silence several times a day, touch my heart, and look up at the sky.

I like to check in with my heart frequently and make sure I am happy.

My heart is my GPS to help me navigate my life.

It never fails to guide me.

HOW THIS LESSON CAN HELP YOU

I believe that a unique road to happiness is given to each of us, special for each person—we just have to listen to our hearts to follow it.

Pause right now.

Put your hand on your heart wherever you are—at home or in a plane or on the way to a train.

Let the noisy world fade a bit.

Ask your heart gently: "Am I happy?"

Your heart will answer, and that will be the beginning of a dialogue that can save your life.

Your heart will help you create a life that brings you happiness you might never have imagined.

Leap . . . With Faith

"There is a tide in the affairs of men which,
taken at the flood, leads on to fortune."
 —*William Shakespeare*

 I was scrunched into coach on a completely full flight. The woman next to me and I had silently agreed to avoid any conversation. It was one of those unspoken bargains: We were both tired.

I pulled my hat down over my eyes and was able to sleep through much of the trip.

She seemed to be doing something with her computer.

When the plane landed in New York, the captain's voice came on: "They say that it is all backed up. They are estimating we have a forty-minute wait before we can get to our gate. Sorry, folks, there's nothing I can do."

We looked at each other.

We decided to talk.

"Not a terrible problem," I said. "At least we are not stuck up in the air."

"Right," she agreed. "Being stuck on the ground is not the worst problem to have when you fly."

We both laughed.

"Sometimes having no problems is the worst problem," she said.

That intrigued me.

"What do you mean?"

"I'm a psychiatrist in Beverly Hills. A lot of my patients are young people. It is kind of my specialty. My husband has a practice that deals primarily with the challenges of growing old, and I have a practice dealing with all the challenges of growing up."

"What are the challenges?" I asked.

"Well, for a lot of my young patients one of their biggest problems is no problems."

"I don't get it," I said, not meaning to be rude but just being honest.

"It's simple. A lot of my patients are children of top movie executives. Their fathers are high achievers and very tough guys. But they overprotect their kids. Let me give you an example. I'll call him Joe Shenk. Joe grows up in Queens. The bad section of Queens. Both his parents work so he has to get himself to school. By age five or at most by ten Joe knows how to survive in pretty mean streets. He can take buses, get around the city, and handle dangerous situations. You get the idea. Then he comes out to Hollywood, makes more money than he ever imagines, and wants to make sure his kids never have to go through the tough times he did. So he has a driver take them to school. They are never without a credit card or fancy clothes or protected environments."

"I get it," I said, and I did.

"Yes," she continued, "it might not sound so bad but the effect is that Joe has *scared* his kids—or, rather, made his kids scared of the outside world."

As she talked and as our plane inched slowly toward the gate, I realized that much the same thing had happened to me.

I had been given so much and protected so much that when my life started to fall apart, I didn't know how to deal with it.

I could never have gotten out of the box I had created for myself had I not leapt forward without *thinking*—with a kind of crazy courage born of desperation.

I had been moving forward for years hoping that if I just dressed up in my Brooks Brothers suit and went out with my briefcase and cell phone as though I were still a big advertising executive, maybe somehow someway I would be given another job at the top of a major international company.

I couldn't face the reality that my former professional life was over forever.

I couldn't move on.

I was strangely passive in the face of such a terrible challenge. I knew I had to change, but I was stuck in a rut. The habit of the familiar—even if it meant failure—was stronger than any effort to exert extra energy in finding a new path.

Robert Frost speaks in his poem "Birches" of the experience when

> . . . *Life is too much like a pathless wood*
> *Where your face burns and tickles with the cobwebs*
> *Broken across it, and one eye is weeping*
> *From a twig's having lashed across it open.*

That's the way I felt as I made myself get up each day but couldn't really figure out how to change the odds in my favor.

I was lost in a wood without knowing how to find a path out. I was failing. The farther I walked, the less progress I seemed to make.

It was as though my life was happening in terrifying slow motion. My depression was weighing me down. My feet were moving as though stuck in quicksand—sinking without knowing how to get out. I was afraid to move too fast or struggle too hard for fear that I might simply drown.

Today, in thinking back to my strangely passive behavior when met with such a personal and professional crisis, I believe it might have had something to do with my early experience with being constantly bullied when I was a young boy.

When I was five years old we moved out to Bronxville, and being new to town, I came to the attention of a bully who attacked me every single day as I tried to make my way to school.

He'd hit me and throw me down, pushing my face into the cold snow so that I could hardly breathe. I would remain as quiet as I could. I learned that if I was quiet and did nothing the pain would—eventually, although every second seemed like hours—cease.

After a few terrible minutes of this torture he would leave me and I would get up, brush my tears away, straighten my clothes, pick up my books—now covered with snow—and go on to school.

I told no one about these horrible daily encounters with the bully. I was embarrassed. I felt it was my fault.

Later in life I reacted to bullies at work in the same way.

If a Ford client would yell at me in a meeting, I would stay calm, quiet, and try to let the storm pass. Often, it worked. But at the cost of subduing my natural feelings.

I feel now that my early habit of passively dealing with aggression and keeping my own true feelings hidden made it harder for me to understand what I should do when a real personal crisis struck.

It was fine to be passive when everything was going well.

When things went badly and I was fired and had to go out on my own and try to re-create and reinvent myself, I found myself stuck in the same-old passive mode—afraid to change and even afraid to complain.

When I went on the Donny Deutsch show to talk about *How*

Starbucks Saved My Life, he summed my struggles up with this perceptive line: "You didn't know what to do because you had been given everything all your life."

He was right. Because I had been *given* everything, I didn't know how to *get the things that mattered most to me.*

Thinking about it now, I realize that this condition is not unique to me. Many of my "trust fund baby" friends have led relatively aimless lives just because they were never forced to go out and get what was best for them.

I remember Hanson Witheridge, who was from an old New England family, whose father had married the heiress to a big oil fortune. I first saw him on the street in New Haven. In those days—the 1960s—New Haven was a rather bleak city. Yet Hanson positively shone. He was wearing a bright blue cashmere sweater and standing by the side of a shiny new silver Porsche. This was a young man who had seemingly been given everything he wanted. But as it would come to pass, he never was forced to examine what his heart truly desired and make the leap to get it.

I have never forgotten that image of him next to his car in New Haven.

Hanson eventually tried his hand at taking pictures, and at one point he decided he would like to be a professional photographer. Hanson came to see me many years later, knowing that as a creative director I could assign photographers to different accounts. He had also heard that I was at the time working with the famous photographer Richard Avedon on a Christian Dior campaign. The campaign had been very well received.

I was happy to see Hanson—although he had aged badly. He looked in his thirties like he could be in his fifties. He had lost most of his hair and acquired a lot of lines in his face (I guessed it was because of his chain-smoking), which changed him from a handsome young man to a person with a prematurely aged face.

He smoked nonstop in my office. He pulled out some photographs he had taken. I could not tell whether they were any good, so I set up an appointment with an art director on the Ford account for him.

At that time Ford was thinking about doing a campaign with great photos of their cars in the most famous spots in America: Times Square, the Golden Gate Bridge, and so on, and I thought Hanson might be hired to help.

Gerry Linkens, one of my top art directors, saw a selection of photographs that Hanson brought in and told me: "He's not bad. I told him to take some shots of the famous New York landmarks and get back to me."

Weeks went by, and Hanson never came back.

Some other person, with less of a personal fortune to fall back on, would have been shooting the next day, and back at least a few days later with a full portfolio of shots. This could have been Hanson's big break. But he was not that kind of person. To some degree, like me, he had been given so much, he really didn't know how to behave when offered a new opportunity.

Too much money can be just as dangerous and terrible as too little.

So these reasons—my early habit of being passive in the face of a bullies, my lack of street sense about what to do when you were out in reality—it was very hard for me to move forward.

I was stuck, and did not know what to do.

As I described earlier in this book, feeling that my life was over, I went back to the old neighborhood where I had grown up. I was trying to recapture some of that positive feeling of being a favored son. The sun was not out that day, and I felt even more discouraged by the reminder of how far I had fallen from my early start at the top of the American Dream.

But I noticed there was a Starbucks store, brightly lit on the gloomy March day. I love coffee and decided to stop in for a latte. Purely by accident I had wandered into a Starbucks that was having a "hiring event," when managers would come from around New York City to hire people for their stores.

I got my latte and then just happened to sit down next to a young African-American woman who was a manager and needed to hire somebody. Her name was Crystal, and I learned later that she had grown up with none of the advantages I had always taken for granted. She was born into the worst kind of poverty. Her mother had died of a drug overdose when she was fifteen. She was sent to live with an aunt who didn't like her. She had made her way in a tough environment and learned how to succeed in the real world in a way I never could imagine.

Now she turned to me.

"Would you like a job?" she asked.

I replied, "YES!" *without* thinking.

At that very moment, that very small word with such a big meaning was the key to turning my life around. My life had reached an all-time low, and I would never have gotten out of my box if I hadn't leapt at her "irrational" offer.

Leaping forward with faith rather than huddling in fear is key to how I turned my life around.

I had never in my life imagined that I would be so eager to trade my Brooks Brothers suit for a green apron, serving others coffee.

If I had thought about it for even a few seconds in a "rational" way, I might well have rejected Crystal's offer.

But I didn't *think* about my answer with my head. I just answered the truth, from my heart.

By answering YES! I was able to begin a new and happier life.

I had to give up thinking I could ever be a big-shot advertising guy again. I see now that not until I had lost enough—virtually lost everything—to be free of the past could I move to the future.

Yet Crystal could not even have moved forward to help save me if I had still been huddling in fear.

If I had frowned at her and shook my head "NO!" and arrogantly dismissed her offer as beneath my great sense of my high status, I would still be stuck in my unhappy box, descending rapidly but not being able to figure out what else to do.

I had to leave my fear and habit of reacting passively to bad events.

I had to move from passively accepting everything I was given to being willing to move forward to get something on my own.

I had to get in touch with my true emotions and not let my head conquer my gut.

People have told me that they have learned from my story: You can't *think* your way out of a box. (And we *all* get stuck in baffling boxes at every age and stage of life.)

To get out of a situation that is trapping you and is not working you have to leap, taking a spontaneous chance to move forward to a whole new world—and leap with the faith that you will land on your feet.

When you leap with faith—rather than huddling in a corner, inactive and incapacitated with fear—others can begin to help you. When you move forward, others can also move forward to help you on your way.

My story is irrefutable proof that forward motion is better than lack of motion.

I discovered that almost any job is better than no job. Just by taking my job at Starbucks, my whole life began to take on a new excitement and energy. Especially fulfilling is a job like mine, where I am challenged in a rejuvenating way with entirely new situations every day.

Doing anything for the first time is almost like being born again to life.

Remember your first day of school?

Or the first day of your first job?

We all respond to those kinds of new experiences with a rush of adrenaline that can chase away stale fears like a breath of fresh air.

Just last March I was invited to speak at the first ever Tucson book fair. What an encouraging sign it is in these hard times that different cities are having success with exciting community events that celebrate reading.

There were thousands of people at the event, and many came up to me afterward to tell their stories about how they had leapt to new lives and were happier than ever.

One young woman who was a volunteer (at most such book fairs, the volunteers are essential to making it all happen) drove me to the airport after the talk.

"I leapt out of my life in Detroit," she said, "and just moved here to Tucson. My husband was a good guy but he had a drinking problem. And a hitting problem. We had talked about having kids but then it suddenly got to me: What kind of role model was I going to be if I stayed with a guy who mistreated me? So I just left.

"I didn't know anyone here but I got a job in a McDonald's. Now I manage my store. You know something? People laugh when I tell them but I am happier managing a McDonald's and living here in Tucson than I ever was back home in the North."

Another couple came up to me when I was signing books.

"Thanks for your story," they told me. "We lost our home in Katrina and decided to leap somewhere—just like you describe.

We didn't think much about the move—we just made the move. We landed here—and boy are we happy we did!"

That same day a lady told me: "I was a big mockery-muck at a Silicon Valley company. I just got tired of all that stress. I moved down here and now I volunteer for the local hospital. It's a lot more rewarding to help patients than it was to try to get computer programmers to get things done on time!"

So many people today are forced to leap without looking, and it *is* frightening. But the most surprising and wonderful thing is so many are finding that their new lives bring them satisfaction they never would have expected.

I—and others—have found that having a job that is based on using your energy to serve others rather than worrying about yourself is a special kind of blessed therapy when you are facing hard times.

If you leap forward with faith there will be angels of grace—like Crystal was for me—eager to catch you and help you.

HOW THIS LESSON CAN HELP YOU

We all live with some fears of the future, but these negative worries can fill our heads and freeze our forward motion—we must replace them with a confident faith.

If you are stuck in a difficult situation and don't know what to do, you now know you should take some action.

Any action is better than inaction.

The very word *emotion* has motion in it.

Trust your emotions rather than trying to judge a new opportunity with your head—and go for it.

Move forward confidently, and your faith will help you create a better future.

You will find that once you have started your forward motion, others will help you on your way.

Let . . . Yourself Be Helped

"Ask and it shall be given unto you."
   —*The Bible*

 Because I had been given so much from an early age, I didn't really know how to ask for help.

I was a proud person. I was so embarrassed to find I needed assistance in life that the very act of asking for help felt like public humiliation.

Now, having gone through my fall from privilege to a better, more realistic life, I know that asking for help is to be humble in the best sense of that word.

Everyone needs help in some way every day.

Crystal once told me: "The biggest single mistake new Partners make is that they don't ask for help enough!"

Asking others for help binds you with the universal desire to get better, to heal.

If you don't ask for help when you most need it, you risk remaining stuck in your own world of hurt.

Once you ask for help, you might be surprised by how much the sunshine of another person's helping spirit can warm your world.

When I first met Crystal she casually handed me a job application form. I looked at the form with horror. I had been *given* my advertising job by Jim Brewster, a Skull & Bones club mate, and during my advertising career I had never had to fill out a job application.

I knew I would fail this first test.

Thankfully, I told Crystal, once again without thinking about it, "I need *your* help." If I hadn't asked Crystal for help, I would have never been able to complete the job application correctly and I would not have gotten the job.

Since then I have also been eager to help others.

In my previous life in advertising I stood by and watched as others struggled with a new challenge.

Today I am eager to help new Partners.

I share my love of coffee with Partners and Guests, for example, and help them to understand why a coffee from Latin America tastes so different from one from Indonesia.

I help take out the garbage, something I am very confident about knowing how to do, and yet I am also quick to ask for help from another barista if I have a complicated new drink to make.

Though I still can't claim that I am the best barista at the espresso bar.

Just the other day a lady came in and asked for a "Double-tall Extra-hot No-foam Latte."

I worked hard to make the milk extra hot with no foam.

I gave her the drink.

She walked away, giving me a smile of thanks.

Seconds later she came back.

"What's the matter?" I asked. "I worked so hard to make it hot enough."

"Mike," she said gently, "you forgot the coffee."

I had forgotten to drop the two espresso shots!

Yet she was very understanding.

I think on some primal level, sharing food and drink is an act of love.

So while Guests are eager to get their drinks, they are also anxious to help make sure the drink is done just right, and they like it when the whole experience can be a source of courtesy and kindness—a loving connection with another human being.

Guests also often ask me for help in understanding all the Starbucks language.

I have discovered that Guests love to say these unusual words, like "Venti" or "Mocha Latte," because for them in their busy, humdrum days, a trip to Starbucks is somewhat like a brief vacation to a foreign country, and the different language itself gives them a psychological break from their workaday worlds.

So today I find it very natural and enjoyable to help my Partners and Guests just as they help me.

It is a rewarding equation . . . a kind of seesaw of positive connection.

Or perhaps you could say that sharing and helping one another is like a kind of gentle, social dance—like a square dance in a country barn in America or a folk dance in a European village that becomes a kind of community event.

Such positive interaction—Partner to Guest, Partner to Partner, Guest to Partner, Guest to Guest—sets up the kind of musical melody of exchanged courtesies that helps make our world a more harmonious place. Helping and being helped is my new way of going through life.

Another way to describe the whole process is that serving others has made me much happier than being served. When I was sitting up in a big corner office, I was isolated. I would call meetings in which the job before us was how to manipulate people into thinking that our brand of car or cereal or chewing gum was better than the other brand.

The differences between cars or kinds of chewing gum would be virtually impossible for even the most loyal consumers to detect, but we would work furiously to make each product seem different.

Our ad meetings remind me of a quote from Shakespeare's *Macbeth*, a play about a couple of ambitious egoists who become disenchanted with a life that does not bring them immediate personal advancement:

> *Tomorrow, and tomorrow, and tomorrow,*
> *Creeps in this petty pace from day to day*
> *Out, out brief candle!*
> *Life's but a walking show, a poor player*
> *That struts and frets his hour on the stage*
> *And then is heard no more: it is a tale*
> *Told by an idiot, full of sound and fury,*
> *Signifying nothing.*

Macbeth and his wife, Lady Macbeth, were so consumed with selfish ambition that they found little satisfaction in life when they weren't triumphing over someone else.

The advertising business was set up in a similar fashion: a slippery slope in which everyone was continually trying to outdo and outcompete the other person. There were few places at the top and it was expected that you would do whatever it took to make it up the greasy pole.

I remember once when a man I worked with, we will call him Russ, went on vacation. By the time he had come back, another colleague of mine, Brian, had successfully taken over his accounts.

We all laughed about it. It was a kind of game to see who could win.

But it is no wonder that kind of game brought so little personal satisfaction.

I have received many letters and e-mails and phone calls from my former colleagues in advertising, and others from those I have never met but who are working hard today in the same business.

All seem to yearn for another kind of life. Art directors want to be artists or film directors. Copywriters wish to be "real" writers or screenwriters.

Few want to continue as they are.

I think the reason is that basic fact that in advertising, you are not devoted to truly helping and serving others. You are simply trying to be as successful as you can on your own.

At Starbucks we work as a team devoted to serving others. There is no hierarchy in the work. Our store manager, who could be seen as our boss, works by our sides and does all the tasks we do: making coffee, getting a mop to clean up spills, making sure the pastries are fresh and the Guests are happy with their experience.

We are called Partners because we work in a partnership of serving others.

There is a kind of powerful therapy in working with a community of like-minded people who are devoted to serving others. There is no time for me or anyone else to focus on our own egos— we are a part of an intense effort to serve others.

It might be called the Zen of service.

Today I have come to believe that human beings are at their happiest when they are thinking of others and finding some way to serve and help each day.

I find so much more satisfaction today even in the most simple acts of service, like bringing someone a good cup of coffee, than I ever did in trying to sell something or trying to advance my own career.

You could say that in my present job I am in the service business. Many people look down at the service business as though being a waiter is below their status.

But serving others can be the greatest gift we have. Especially in the simple ways we can serve one another every day.

Don't you take special notice when someone holds a door open for you or lets you get on the subway car first?

Or lets you speak fully before interrupting?

Don't you notice when the salesperson gives you a smile as she hands you a magazine you picked up at the newsstand?

Simple acts of service can be so fulfilling because I think in the most basic sense, serving one another is what we are on Earth to do.

I hasten to add that you can serve others in many ways. I feel that if you have a talent and share it, that is a kind of service— whatever that talent might be, from singing to writing to being a doctor or a chef or a barista.

There are no limits or rules on how to serve or how to help others. Recently I have met so many people who tell me that they have found the greatest satisfaction in their lives by finding some way to serve.

Last week a person at one of my talks in Florida offered to drive me to the airport. I was happy to accept his help.

On the way he told me his story. Since I have opened my heart to others I have found that others are more anxious to share their lives with me.

"I was diagnosed with leukemia last year," he said.

"I'm sorry," I replied automatically.

"Don't be."

He gave me a quick look.

"That's what I wanted to tell you. I am happier than I have ever been because I have found a way to truly help other people."

"How?"

"Simple. I heard of this village in Guatemala. They needed a new school. I got a friend of mine who is a contractor—I'm an architect by profession—and we went down there to see if we could help."

He laughed. "Boy, did they need help!

"Mainly physical stuff," he continued. "I spent a lot more time carrying bricks and mixing up concrete than I ever did before in my life. But I can't tell you how satisfying it is."

"It's still going on?"

"You bet! I'm going down next week again. We've got the foundation laid and are just beginning the rest. I might not live to see it all finished."

Here he paused. It wasn't easy for him to go on.

"Hey," he finally said, "what I am trying to tell you is that just by helping out this little village I had never even heard of before, I am feeling better about my life and everything."

I have heard stories like his in many forms over the last months of my travels.

Person after person has come up to me after I have talked about the importance of helping and being helped to let me know that they have had the same kind of transformative experience.

Life is so much more fulfilling when you let yourself be helped and find a way to help others.

HOW THIS LESSON CAN HELP YOU

Be humble and feel free to ask for help.

By opening your heart to help, and by helping others, you will find a more fulfilling life and a new path to happiness.

Find a way today to help someone.

Be it ever so small a service, you will find that this willingness to help others will brighten your day.

Look . . . With Respect
at Every Individual You See

"Amazing grace, how sweet the sound
That saved a wretch like me
I once was lost, but now I'm found
Was blind, but now I see."
   —*John Newton, "Amazing Grace"*

 This eighteenth-century hymn sounds a deep truth for me. John Newton, who wrote the words to "Amazing Grace," was a slave trader who finally realized with a terrible shock that his human cargo was full of *individual* souls rather than simply products to be sold.

I don't compare myself to Newton in the sense of having practiced an evil, if legal trade. (Advertising might take advantage of people by encouraging them to buy silly or even unhealthy things, but it is no way comparable to enslaving anyone.) But I have realized that *every* person I met in my life deserved to be seen for who they truly were rather than a target ready to be sold a product if we could make it shine with enough status.

When I was growing up in New York City I was told: "Don't make eye contact!"

I purposely would never even glance at people who appeared to be from different races, classes, or backgrounds than myself.

I avoided subways, for there was no way to avoid the physical crush of coming so close to those I considered not worthy to intrude on my comfort zone. I wore blinders and only wished to see and be with people like me.

The world I grew up in was so privileged and protected that even my own children find it hard to imagine how isolated I was from the "real world."

My tendency to want to be with people just like me was encouraged by my education at Yale. Yale of my day was all male, and the undergraduates were largely from the same group of Wasps (white Anglo-Saxon Protestants) that had founded the school in the eighteenth century. Today Yale is a much different place: full of people from all over America and the world of every gender, race, religion, and economic background.

It probably seems strange to young readers today, but in my time at Yale I was told, implicitly and sometimes explicitly, that we were a favored bunch. An elite group.

Once again, the very idea of being part of an "elite" group has become widely discredited. But in my day it was something to boast about.

My feeling of being above the crowd only grew when I joined the J. Walter Thompson Company. The company actually called itself the University of Advertising, and its halls were filled with Ivy Leaguers. We occupied fancy offices high up in the Graybar Building with handmade iron grills instead of plain doors and had original works by Picasso and Chagall on our walls.

We worked far above the hurly-burly of Grand Central Terminal. Our role was to judge others and assign their value. And we taught ourselves and others to judge people by demographic groups: affluent, young, well-educated, well-dressed people were our favored target groups.

In other words, I spent most of my life judging others based on what they *looked* like and not on what they *were* like.

I was a visual gatekeeper of my own sense of entitlement.

I thank God today that I was yanked out of that blind life. I believe now it was a kind of divine intervention, which I am so grateful for.

Just as the hymn says, "I was blind but now I see."

I *was* blind.

And if I hadn't been fired—thrown out of that cozy, self-congratulatory advertising club—I would never have discovered the whole amazing world outside my blinders. Yet this gift of grace and a chance to begin seeing others face to face rather than as representatives of a class or race would not have been possible for me if I had not truly looked at Crystal when she looked at me. Though she was so different in upbringing, education, race, and age from me, when she talked to me, I truly looked at her. When she asked me if I wanted a job, I put my blinders down, and I looked into her eyes and saw a kind, intelligent, and strong person who might help me.

That sight saved my life.

And Crystal saw me for who I really was as well. On the first day of work, when I stood frozen with fear like a frightened deer in the doorway of her store, Crystal brought me over to a small table and served me delicious coffee and a tasty pastry. In her eyes there was understanding of the shock I was going through. I felt comforted—no longer uncomfortable by the outward differences between us but realizing she *saw* me and knew how afraid I was and was showing me a kind of loving kindness that touched my heart.

Then she introduced me to Kester. In a million years I would never have chosen Kester as my training coach in this new life. When I first saw him he appeared to be the kind of guy I would have crossed the street to avoid: A "do-rag" around his head, earphones plugged in, big, tall, and tough Kester looked dangerous to me.

But I had the courage to look up at him when he came over to the table and see him with fresh eyes. And when he smiled at me I knew that Kester, like Crystal and my other new Partners, would treat me as they would every other individual.

Despite the fact that I was so different from them they treated me with the understanding and mercy that I needed: not because I was different, but, rather, and much more important, because I was simply another struggling soul.

When I would drop a mug of hot coffee or make some other mistake, Kester would tell me "everyone does that" (I learned later that, on the contrary, most new Partners do not make those clumsy mistakes). Kester believed in me without judging me critically because of my advanced age and obvious lack of knowledge of the most basic facts of street life.

To me, each Partner became not a representative of a particular class or "target group"—the way we used to refer to people in advertising—but a real individual.

My Partners in my store all wear green aprons and we share many of the same jobs during every shift, yet each of us is unique and we each have our own individual lives and stories.

Yami, for example, is originally from Panama. Her husband drives a cab. In the last year Yami has gotten pregnant and had a lovely little daughter.

Jim's real love is his life as a drummer. He comes in sleepy after late nights with his band, but he moves faster than anyone in our store. Maybe it's his drumming, but his hand-eye coordination in making drinks is in a league of its own.

When I open with Chris I have to make sure to get there a few minutes before five A.M.—he is always early. And if we are joined by Aya we know she will be meticulous in putting out the freshest morning pastries. Aya is leaving us to work for a Starbucks store in the city at a location that makes it easier to get to her apartment and her college classes.

Magdalena just got back from visiting her family in Poland. She is working hard, balancing Starbucks shifts with demanding assignments at school.

Lani is a single mother who gained forty pounds and then lost forty pounds after the birth of her handsome son.

Carmella comes from a small village in Italy, and her two sons also worked at Starbucks when they were going to college.

Matt is a gregarious guy who is devoted to his young daughters and is able to connect with virtually every Guest who comes in.

Jonathan is one of the tallest Partners in our store. Well over six feet two, he brings a big, positive presence to every shift when he is there.

Jordan is not as big but has an intense dedication to every single job that helps remind me to keep my focus. Rachel has a large smile that reminds me not to get too intense! And Margaret is able to handle the mysteries of money and give me the proper tip each week.

Tasha, my current store manager, has a soothing style—even if I come to her to ask for her help with my schedule when she's in the midst of other, more stressful situations. Tasha projects a sense of confidence that everything will turn out well—which makes me and our Partners feel confident as well.

Martin is our Partner and has become our district manager (DM). Before he became our DM he was manager of my Bronxville store and helped me make the move from the city. Working with

Martin, I am carried along by his passion for making sure our store will really sparkle in every way—by cleaning every inch so it shines and by sharing his big smile and warm welcome with every Guest who walks in the door.

And all our regular Guests are as unique as my Partners.

Billy, who now drives a taxi in town (after playing semipro golf and working as a top executive in the sporting world), is always first in the door when we open at 5:30 A.M.

Billy is full of good humor and makes a point of giving us an extra-large tip to start our day.

Vincent is the best-dressed Guest at 6:30 A.M. Vinnie will get a Venti Latte for himself and a Venti Coffee for his wife.

Frank shows up at the same time in his pajamas for his first Quad Nonfat Latte of the day. Frank will be back later for another Latte—beautifully dressed this time—before he rides into New York or flies to Amsterdam, staying on top of his busy textile business.

Lisa works long hours on Wall Street, but she never misses her Venti Coffee—bold—to start her day.

Alex also has little time to spare. She is on the way to doing her broadcast news from a studio in the city. Christina is on her way to the city, but she's on her way to help in a hospital. Elise is a doctor and also heads into Manhattan after stopping—very briefly—at our store. (This despite the fact that there is a Starbucks on the ground floor of her hospital!)

Nancy was an actress and is now a full-time Bronxville mom very involved in making sure all her kids get the best education they can at the local public school. She is part of a group of moms who drop in after dropping their kids off at school, and they always seem to be sharing a table that is filled with the sound of laughter.

Connie was born in Greece and comes in after working out at

the local gym with a special smile for us to get her "reward": a Grande Nonfat Latte.

Lou has a Tall Coffee "on the rocks," as he says, meaning with a few cubes of ice to cool it off. I am one of the few old enough to remember his expression from my drinking days. After my shift I will sometimes sit with Lou and share some memories of drinking with Frank Sinatra and Toots Shor in the glory days of bars in New York.

One of our favorite Guests is a tea drinker. Mike Duffy will have a Venti Tea and nurse it gently during the day. He is a kind fellow who is so at peace with himself and the world that he gives our whole store a sense of serenity.

Blaise was unemployed when I first met him a couple of years ago and then got a job teaching in one of New York's most challenging schools. He loves it.

Maria is also a dedicated teacher and comes in early to have a coffee to start her busy day. She is never in too much of a hurry to make a point of calling my Partners and me by name and wishing each of us a cheerful "Good morning!"

When I truly opened my eyes I could see the unique light of a God-given spirit in every individual I met.

Each spirit was different from mine and from every other soul.

Taking my blinders off revealed a marvelous variety of individuals. Today I know that every individual I see has the potential to uplift my life. There is a primal truth to the cliché "Variety is the spice of life." When we open our eyes, this variegated universe is such a delight. This October, I have been amazed at the beauty of each individual leaf that falls from the sky or that rustles at my feet as I walk.

I now have come to believe that we are all meant to create unique lives. No one should live or *look* exactly like me or anyone else!

Each individual should reflect his or her own special vision and spirit in life.

Today I happily and gratefully make eye contact with *every* individual I see.

What a great gift that open sight is to me!

HOW THIS LESSON CAN HELP YOU

As you walk along the street today, be sure to make eye contact with people you pass on your way.

You will see the unique light behind the eyes of everyone you greet.

Remember: We are not what we look like but what we are like.

LESSON 6

Learn . . . From Your Children

"I hear America singing."

—*Walt Whitman*

 Last year I learned from my daughter Laura how to turn idealistic dreams into practical realities.

In January I was able to share an historic night with her in Washington, D.C., at a "staff party" at Obama's inauguration. I was there because I had helped my daughter, who had become one of his organizers, to canvass and call and make sure people turned out to vote on Election Day.

Obama took the stage without any notes or teleprompter. It was just Obama and about a thousand or so young people, most in their early twenties—and me.

Laura had been given a ticket for herself and a ticket for one guest to this party for "staff only," and she gave her precious extra ticket to me.

Surrounding us, standing shoulder to shoulder, were the youth brigade, who had worked and organized around the clock for months and even years to help get Obama elected. It was his last inaugural party, and he and Michelle were clearly relaxed and happy to be there. Michelle took a seat on the stage. Obama picked up a handheld microphone and walked to the front of the stage as though he wanted to be closer to everyone.

The crowd was cheering and clapping. You could feel the relief and happiness. Like my daughter, they had put their lives on hold, left family and friends, and had been working so hard for this moment. Now here he was. Now "Mr. President."

But as soon as Obama spoke his first words, the exuberant, noisy crowd suddenly fell silent. I was reminded of how disciplined they really were. These weren't hippy idealists like my Woodstock generation, so ready to "drop out" of the real world. Laura and her friends were practical people; rather gentle people who wanted the world to be a better place. They had the focused, disciplined energy that my generation had sadly lacked.

The campaign had appealed to Laura's character in a powerful way. From the earliest age she would grow impatient at what she saw as any unfairness. Her friends at school were invariably those she felt needed her help. Laura was a great listener—rare in our family. She was sympathetic to the burden of discrimination against all minorities and hated any sense of injustice.

As she grew older she had less and less patience with any jokes or snide remarks I might make about anyone who had fewer advantages. For much of my privileged life I believed I deserved all my good fortune.

She would tell me: "Dad, you just don't get it. You were *born* with everything!"

So when she saw me working at Starbucks—watching how hard I had to struggle just to keep up in every area of the business with people who had never been given a Yale education or any other benefits—she had been pleased.

"Dad," she told me the first day she came to see me during my shift, "you are finally getting it."

Laura realized that I had come to respect people of every

background. So when she asked me to help her with her mission of electing Obama, I leapt at the chance.

Before joining the campaign she had been a teacher in Philadelphia. She left that role for what she thought was a chance to change the odds for the less fortunate and help those with fewer advantages.

I was amazed when I visited Laura at the office she had helped set up for Obama. Clustered around her desk were about thirty middle-aged white men. Laura was giving them the instructions about where to canvass that night. The campaign liked volunteers in an area to visit their neighbors, answer their questions about Obama, and hopefully get them to vote for him.

Laura sent me out with some of these volunteers from largely Republican neighborhoods.

"Your daughter is amazing," I was told. "Not only is she working so hard, she has done a great job of *efficiently* organizing this whole thing."

These were men who had major jobs in top American companies and they respected efficiency and hard work. I was amazed that Laura, who could be so humble and retiring, had moved forward with such a sure sense of command. Now she was at the inauguration party to celebrate an unlikely victory after all that hard work.

Newly elected President Obama looked out over the crowd, so quiet, expectant.

"You're so young!" he said.

A great roar of laughter greeted his remark—delivered as though he couldn't believe what he was seeing.

I was impressed at how Obama hadn't blinked before he stated that surprising truth. You could see that, as he looked out over all those upturned faces, he was truly astonished at how *young* they were.

Another politician might not have had the guts to speak that truth because it might have sounded negative to them. But Obama was not there to condescend to them. He was there to acknowledge the incredible reality.

"You've cleaned up a lot since Iowa," he said, and here they roared and applauded as much for themselves as for him.

My daughter Laura and her boyfriend and all their friends had indeed made a special effort to put on ties and dresses that night. Laura looked so beautiful.

As the laughter died down Obama said: "You didn't know it couldn't be done. You didn't know you couldn't get five-dollar donations on the Internet," he said. "You didn't know you couldn't just open a Web site in Idaho and then send me an e-mail saying you were organizing the state for me!"

My daughter and her friends laughed. They recognized how crazy and improbable the whole thing had been and how creative they had been.

"You didn't know you couldn't do it—so you just did it!"

Here the yells and happy shouts turned into the anthem and mantra and song of the campaign.

A thousand young throats started chanting: "YES WE CAN, YES WE CAN, YES WE *CAN*!"

Laura and her friends loved music and the Internet, and she told me they played the YouTube version of the Will.i.am song "Yes We Can," which became their anthem, several times a day.

I was with Laura at her Obama headquarters office when her team gathered with other neighborhood volunteers to watch the first debate with McCain. Before the debate everyone got soft drinks and brownies and then sat and watched the "Yes We Can" YouTube song, singing along.

This was their marching song, their "Star-Spangled Banner," their "Song of Marseille," their generation's "We Shall Overcome."

But for them it hadn't turned out to be "someday." That night they had brought that vision of hope home and changed America.

The whole huge hall of the Washington, D.C., armory rocked as they roared what had become a victory chant:

"YES WE CAN!"

"Yes, you could!" Obama said and, hearing him speak, the crowd died down, chanting, "And YES, YOU CAN!"

The powerful chant started up, but Obama raised his hand, and the room fell silent. This was a group of "kids" that had a sense of crowd control I had never seen before. One minute they were yelling and whooping like revolutionaries storming the barricades, and the next instant, with a gesture from Obama, you could hear the scrape of Laura's shoe as she adjusted her position to see him better.

Obama stopped smiling.

"Look," Obama said, "don't let them *ever* take that away from you. *You* helped make this country better, this world better. Don't ever let anybody ever tell you *you can't*!"

At this another cheer went up. But Obama wasn't finished. He raised his hand for quiet again. He seemed to me at this point almost like a stern father rather than a man enjoying a huge accomplishment. He wasn't there just to ride the wave of their approval. I realized at that instant that Obama is not the kind of politician or the kind of person simply interested in popularity or the approval of crowds. *He's a teacher,* I suddenly thought. Teaching is what he loves to do. I remembered he was a professor of law.

"Don't wait for another four years," Obama told them. "Don't wait for another election. Don't wait two years. Don't wait two months . . . or two weeks. Tomorrow, whatever you do, whatever job you do or neighborhood you live in, remember what you have done: and remember that can make *your* neighborhood a better place."

I could see Laura and her friend nodding their heads as Obama made his points. I realized that whatever Obama accomplished as president—whether he was successful or not in all the change he wanted to achieve for America—he had had *already changed Laura and her friends' lives forever.*

Obama stood, still smiling, happy, proud of them for all that had been done. Realizing this was not the place for a serious lecture, he just couldn't resist adding one more piece of fatherly advice: "Don't ever forget: You *can* change the world!"

But by this time Obama's words were just part of a great wave of joyous sound—Laura and her friends had waited and worked too long to stop the cheering now.

Michelle stood up. Obama took her hand. They were getting ready to leave the stage. Most of these young people might never see the Obamas so close again.

I noticed that Laura's hazel eyes were glistening with tears. This was it. The moment they had worked so hard for. Many like Laura had thought despite all their hard work, such a triumph—like so many hopeful dreams—might never happen. Even tonight many were in a state of disbelief that they had really helped pull off this surprising victory.

"I love you too!" he called, one last time, and then he and Michelle were gone—surrounded by the new president's big security guard.

The roar continued. Not just for seconds. For *minutes.*

I had never known Laura to be into such popular demonstrations, but now she and her friends were shouting their hearts out, celebrating what they all knew was one of the greatest experiences of their lives. And *my* life. It occurred to me at that historic moment that if it hadn't been for my daughter, I wouldn't have been even a small part of this new spirit.

I quietly pledged to myself that night that even an old guy

like myself—decades older than anyone else in the room—could to try to make the world a better place—starting with my own job and my own neighborhood, just as Obama had advised us.

Whatever Obama does or doesn't do as president—and I am certain as someone who has lived through so many messed-up administrations—he will make his fair share of errors. Yet he has already changed my life.

And I would never have had the experience if I hadn't been willing to learn from my daughter. Learning from Laura has been one of the greatest educational experiences of my life.

In fact, I realize now I have learned valuable life lessons from all my children.

I have learned from my oldest daughter, Bis, the value of combining a belief in the value of hard work with a great sense of humor and a dedication to an art form that is never easy. Against all odds Bis has directed and written some wonderful films.

She was happy to start as a hardworking "gopher" for Martin Scorsese when she was just out of NYU film school. She was able to find a way to work with the dramatic and ever-demanding Miramax boys. She even once introduced me to their wonderful mother Miriam.

And by being willing to do anything—from running errands to helping set up Hollywood parties to helping publicize the movie *The Crying Game*, Bis was given a chance to direct her own film. All that hard work paid off.

Bis's film, which she wrote and directed, is called *Goldfish Memories*, a romantic comedy about how quickly people can forget and renew love, and that, finally, finding true love is an act of faith that requires an ability to stay constant and true in every sense of the word.

The title comes from the fact that goldfish are reputed to lose their memory so quickly that with one turn of their fishbowl, they see everything as new.

From my daughter Annie, who is an actress, I have learned to have courage: She is fearless in showing up at audition after audition and appearing in off-Broadway show after off-Broadway show, despite the terrifying odds of getting to perform on *any* stage in the fiercely competitive city of New York.

Once Annie was in a middle-school production of *Our Town*. As soon as she came onstage and began to speak, it was as though a luminous spirit lit up the stage. Annie's powerful, positive presence drew every eye to her. She was an immediate "showstopper."

I was so eager to share her limelight that I went backstage and asked Mr. Good, who was the teacher in charge of such productions, if he would find a role for me to play with Annie.

In Annie's next show, he found a role for me—a country doctor.

I was so excited.

But opening night, I was a flop.

In my nervous state on the stage, I forgot half my lines. Fortunately, Annie had learned my part as well as her own and carried me through our brief scene together. But that was another great lesson for me: Just because you share some of the same genes with your children does not mean you have got their special gifts yourself.

My son Charles is another good example of that to me.

From Charles I have learned the importance of doing what you want to do with a kind of gentle grace. He teaches at a farm school in Massachusetts, where kids from the inner city come out and spend several days actually living and working and helping produce organic, natural food. "A lot of these kids have never really seen a blue sky before," Charles says. "At first they go crazy— just racing around the fields. Then they come with me on my chores and learn how to help feed our pigs or make a fresh batch of maple syrup."

Charles is fair, firm, and fun with the young students who visit his farm high in the hills.

He has a gift, teaching without condescending to these kids who are much younger than him. They catch his love of the outdoor world, with all its natural seasons and harvests. It has been an inspiration to me.

I have also learned a lot from his ability to stay in sync with the natural forces of life and maintain a quiet sense of pacing in the world.

I went up to spend a night with Charles a couple of months ago. The next day I was racing through the scrambled eggs he made me. "Don't rush, Dad," Charles said. "Those eggs were created by our chickens to enjoy . . . slowly."

I have always eaten as fast as possible. Charles helps me remember to savor every bite.

Charles reminds me that all our food is the result of care and interaction with the natural world all around us and should therefore be treated with true appreciation.

From my youngest child, Jonathan, I have learned the joys of a fresh and original imagination. As Jonathan has grown older—much too fast, he is over six years old now—he has become more and more talented at turning every kind of situation into a new adventure. Every hour of his day is filled with a kind of imaginative storytelling: trains, cars, or the shift of the clouds in the sky are reasons to fill his heart and mind and soul with wonder and a new sense of what might be possible, and he comes up with a new narrative for every scene. Cars will crash, trains will ride through storms, storms themselves will cause an ambulance to rush to the rescue of a family on the side of a river rising through the rain—every dramatic scene he conjures up in his mind seems to set off a new story line for Jonathan. He has shown me that life can be so much more fun when lived as a spontaneous, creative experience.

All my children have also shown me the great gift of not judging others or even judging what one does in life, but moving forward to embrace life itself in all its swirling creativity.

I feel in these last years that I have learned more from my children than I ever did in a stuffy Yale classroom or a hermetically sealed corporate office.

You can learn from all children—whatever your relationship is. You can learn from nephews and nieces and grandchildren, as well as the children of friends who happen to enter your life during the course of a day or an entire lifetime.

HOW THIS LESSON CAN HELP YOU

Stop advising your children about life for a moment and learn from them. Children often have a new approach to life that can help you find a new way to live.

Learn . . . From Your Father

"The first rule of life is to have a good time.
There is no second rule."
—*Brendan Gill*

 I learned many valuable life lessons from my father. Even in his death he never stopped teaching me.

We had a memorial service for him that seemed to bring forth a whole host of happy memories that gave me new strength to go forward with my life.

It is one of the strange and wonderful things of life that somehow my father is with me more now in so many ways than he ever was before. Although his body has gone, his effervescent spirit is a more powerful presence than ever. Such was the uplifting feeling when we gathered to give him a final earthly celebration. My father died more than ten years ago, but the joyous, celebratory service is still fresh in my memory.

In his later years my father had attended many such services, and he had a few rules:

1. Let no one speak who cannot speak well.
2. Keep it short—the shorter the better.
3. Make it funny. Death wins if you take him too seriously.

I remember my father delivering eulogies for rather august and serious people that would have the whole church or temple rocking with laughter.

We had the memorial celebration for him in the Town Hall Theater in New York, and we worked hard to make sure that it would be such a happy experience for all.

We invited all his friends from all his many worlds: *The New Yorker* magazine, where he had worked for more than sixty years; the preservation and conservation friends he had battled with to save the best of his beloved city; friends from the literary and theater worlds; his immediate family and the many "honorary" family members he embraced; his old college friends; and also—most important—the general public.

My father always championed the idea of nonexclusivity for the citizens of his beloved city. He would have loved the fact that *everyone* was invited to his free celebration.

It was a great show.

My father had always loved to speak, and he spoke with a rare eloquence and positive power. The speakers at his service were in the same grand tradition.

George Plimpton, the founder, editor, and publisher of the literary magazine *The Paris Review*, the author of many best-selling books and who appeared in several great movies such as *Good Will Hunting*, brought the house to its feet with his wonderful picture of my father in his element in heaven.

"I can see Brendan at a boardinghouse in heaven called The Hedges," George began.

There was laughter at this, for most of the audience remembered my father saying and writing that he would like to die—if he ever had to go—"leaping over a hedge."

One of the lessons my father demonstrated to me by his energetic example was that if you were going to walk, then maybe you should run! He loved the idea that life should be lived with an almost maniacal physical and mental forward motion, and he lived it that way every day.

My father taught me that life should be lived always leaning forward toward the next, exciting adventure. One example: My father couldn't stand organized games, but his old friend Jay Laughlin, who had founded the publishing house New Directions and was a neighbor in Norfolk, insisted on getting him out to play golf on the weekends my father was in the country. Because of his love for Jay, my father would agree to spend some time on the golf course with him. Yet to see my father play golf was to understand his passion for nonstop forward motion. He would literally run from one shot to another, pausing only briefly to hit his ball and chase it on its way.

My father's whole attitude about how life must be lived can be summed up in this couplet by the poet Andrew Marvell:

> *Thus, though we cannot make our Sun*
> *Stand still, yet we will make him run!*

The very idea that he wanted to be leaping over a hedge to leave life was symbolic of the courageous and joyous way my father had chosen to meet his greatest challenges.

George went on to say that he could see my father at The Hedges boardinghouse in heaven—which would, of course, be full of other literary lions—lecturing every other author about how to live and how to write.

"I can see Brendan happily lecturing Henry James," George said, "on how to *get on* with the story—was there anyone who could write with Brendan's speed or dash? Was there anyone who was more impatient with pompous airs? I am also sure Brendan will not resist asking Edith Wharton about how it was to live and write in the highest reaches of society in old New York. Did anyone—ever—love social life as much, and the very idea of parties as the very best place to experience life?"

"Brendan," George concluded, "would have brought a whole new dimension of life and laughter to heaven."

The audience laughed with happy recognition of my father's immortal passion for literature and for being part of the most exciting social swim at the very same time.

My father's life was a lesson to anyone aspiring to an artistic life: You did not necessarily have to exist like a hermit to create great works of art. You did not need to hide away in an "ivory tower." My father proved by his example that you could be a great writer and still be a passionate participant in life.

George finished his eulogy by recalling how much of his time and heart my father had devoted to saving—and encouraging others to save—New York City:

"Brendan was a Pied Piper of preservation. Before Brendan came along we New Yorkers had been always so proud of tearing the past down as quickly as we could. Yet Brendan was able to create a popular cause where none had been before. No one has ever been able to make saving a city so much damn fun!"

Here the audience not only laughed but applauded. My father had brought a revolutionary zeal and appeal to the very act of saving the great built heritage of New York.

I remembered—as I recounted in *How Starbucks Saved My Life*—when I was working as a creative director of J. Walter Thompson's Washington office, and my father asked for my help in making sure there was lots of publicity for his effort to save Grand Central by bringing the case before the Supreme Court. We helped organize a train trip down to Washington. It was amazing fun. My father and Jackie Onassis walked up and down the cars, speaking with everyone—and you could hear the laughter ripple across the passengers as my father moved from group to group.

I invited all the powerful luminaries in Washington to meet the train when it arrived at Union Station. No one turned down my invitations. It was a wonderful party, and once again Jackie and my father were able to woo and win every V.I.P. they met—including the vice president and the wife of a Supreme Court justice.

They won the Supreme Court case, helped by the great amount of goodwill they had generated with the key decision makers and the fact that the story of their cause and their train trip was covered as a major news event in all the mass media. Jackie and my father had made Saving Grand Central a popular cause to support.

My father was an example of how devoting a large part of your life to a good cause as a responsible and caring citizen of your community can also be an enjoyable experience. My father's lesson is that good deeds can be combined with good times.

He showed that success comes faster for any social activity devoted to the public good when you can make it something the public itself looks forward to and enjoys.

In his younger days, before he became so famous and long before he had been able to convince the mayor or any other "powers that be" that saving the city was a worthy mission, my father would go into New York City on Sunday afternoons and conduct "walking tours" of the oldest sections. When I got to be about fifteen years old he would sometimes take me on these Sunday-afternoon excursions. There might be a dozen other people with him. There would be a few architects my father knew and a child or two along with their parents. Seeing this small gathering, hearing my father's beautiful baritone voice filling the air with such conviction and enthusiasm, even a few tourists might join us.

I remember one afternoon we were outside St. Ann's Church

in Brooklyn when my father was gesturing toward the sky and saying with a voice that rose with volume as though he were addressing a much larger crowd: "This is the most beautiful structure under . . . heaven!" A little old man and his wife stared with astonishment at the sight of this young, passionate man so publicly and joyfully extolling a building they had probably barely noticed. Their mouths literally fell open. They joined our group for rest of the day. At the end of the "tour" the man shook my father's hand and I heard him say: "I never knew I lived in such an impressive neighborhood before!"

My father didn't care to whom he was proselytizing. He was not picky in his desire to share his mission for preservation—so rare in that era of the 1950s when he first began to make people realize its importance. My father's gregarious energy, his admiration for the beautiful buildings, and his love for the history of his favorite city was a passion that could capture the imagination even of a stranger on a Sunday afternoon. Soon a large crowd would be following a young man they did not even know—drawn by the power of his words and a desire to share his devotion to preserving the endangered beauty of the past.

Don't we all remember with fondness those teachers we encountered as we went through school who swept us away with their love of their subject? My father was an exemplar of that lesson: If you share a subject you love with others, they can learn to love it too.

In his love for preserving and celebrating the best of New York he created a whole new kind of cause that gained momentum as he devoted more and more time to sharing his vision.

He was a kind of irresistible force in helping make popular a cause so few had shared before. Yet his passion for preservation of the great architecture of the past was just one of the many gifts that he shared so generously with the world.

My father taught me yet another lesson: Each of us is given *many* talents that can be developed and widely shared. While my father called architecture his "first love," he devoted his career to his writing talent and creating great literature.

At the memorial service, John Guare, author of *Six Degrees of Separation* and many other hit plays and movies, declared that my father's first novel, *The Trouble of One House*, "should be read by everyone here today. It is one of the great American novels and sadly neglected."

My father would have been immensely pleased by John's accolade. He had worked for a decade on his heartrending story of a family facing the death of a beloved mother—the same tragic trauma my father had experienced when he was growing up. It was a work of fiction in which my father was brave enough to tell the deeper truth about the searing and seminal event of his childhood. Although it was a critical success, winning a National Book Award, my father's first novel never became popular. It did not become anything near a bestseller. My father was very disappointed that all his hard work and courage in exposing the pain he had long kept hidden was not rewarded with more popular recognition. He never attempted to write such a painful, soul-searching novel again. For my father once described himself as "having a fatal desire to please." He once told me that this need to win recognition was so strong, it made him seek the applause of an audience rather than be faithful to the best of his talent—which he saw as writing a great work of fiction.

My father found the actual act of writing lonely. If he was going to write, he wanted to feel sure that he would be acclaimed. As I near seventy, I remember vividly how at my father's seventieth birthday party he made this public promise: "Now at this late stage of my life, I am going to leave the stage. Give up my public committees and retire to write. Write. Write. Write. That's how I am going to spend my remaining years."

It wasn't to turn out that way. The pull of the need to please and be appreciated was too strong, and the need for his presence to save the city he so loved was also too great. My father continued to spend much of his life in the public eye—serving the public good and also having a wonderful time at very public parties.

Yet I remember talking with him in what turned out to be our last conversation as we waited for a train at the Bronxville Station.

"Busy day?" I asked.

"Yes, I've got too much to do. I have meetings at the Municipal Art Society and the Andy Warhol Foundation. I wish I could just write. I have so much more to . . ."

He let the thought trail off. He seemed a bit frustrated with how his life had gotten away from him. Starting as a teenager at Kingswood School he dreamed of being a great poet and writer. At Yale his dream had continued and grown. Now in his last years he was still pursuing his goal.

Although he had written many wonderful books, my father, like many great artists and high achievers I have known, was never happy with his performance. It is like the irritation of the sand in the oyster that produces the pearl. Most great artists are always tormented by the idea that they must do more.

One of the most important life lessons I learned from my father is that one shouldn't be afraid to strive for something more—at any age.

I knew on that last morning we spent together that my father was still frustrated that he had—at least in his own eyes—not yet written the "Great American Novel." Yet he was in no way depressed by what he saw as a challenge worthy of his talents.

The ancient Greeks defined life as "the exercise of one's vital powers along lines of excellence in a life affording them scope," and I think that captures my father's eternally questing attitude.

My father lived his whole life searching for ever more excellence in his writing while also embracing his role as a responsible citizen and participant in the larger community of his time.

And his desire to get better and better at the writing craft he loved so much never ceased. I realize now that this was one of the secrets to his amazing energy at every age: My father was always eagerly seeking a more creative and powerful way to share his story with the world.

I knew that morning that my father was going to go into his office and begin to write, once again, the Great American Novel that he had always promised himself.

In his eighties my father was just as happy and confident and determined in his ability to create a great work of art as he had been as a teenage poet growing up in Hartford or as a young writer in New York.

My father—even on that train platform months from his death—was still the youngest person in spirit that I have ever met. As I grew older, my father seemed to grow ever younger.

I remember at my fortieth birthday party my father made a toast: "Gatesy has now passed me in age! He is today much more grown up than I am—or than I ever wish to be!"

My father was right. When I turned forty he still seemed in spirit like a thirty-five-year-old at most, or even, in many ways, like a twenty-five-year-old. I remember leaving my birthday party around eleven o'clock. I was tired. I heard later that my father, surrounded by many of my friends so stimulated by his company, had all stayed up well past l A.M.

As he got older my father also seemed to develop even more speed: He talked faster, wrote faster, and developed a walking style that most would regard as a run. He would dash through the crowds of his city like a broken field runner—focused on squeezing some more positive activity and achievement out of each second of the day.

A vital lesson and a legacy my father gave me are never to give up on actively pursuing your dreams—whatever they may be. He never gave up on trying to write better today than he had yesterday. He was continually in a kind of energized forward motion—happily driven by a goal that was always before him. He probably knew, deep down, that he could never grant himself the satisfaction of believing he had ever achieved it.

But how he loved the uphill effort! He knew that he had been given a rare level of talent and energy, and he shared those gifts so happily with the world.

Although my father liked to pose as a man of great vanity, those who got to know him knew my father was the least self-congratulatory of men. Once I introduced him at a fund-raising event for the library in the little village of Norfolk. By this time in his life my father was incredibly busy and much sought after by many charitable organizations as well as a speaker at major literary events, but he never turned down a worthwhile request to help the local library raise money.

My father dismissed my idea that it was any sacrifice for him to be there on that rainy afternoon in a small country town (although I knew that day he had just flown back from England and had driven up from the city to be there). "I'm no saint. This library is the heart of our community. My heart is always won by books. What better cause could *any* writer have than to support the place that values words? I would love the idea that some day—far, far into the future, I hasten to add—a young boy or girl might reach up high on a dusty shelf in this beautiful space"—my father gestured around the hundred-year-old room that held so many volumes—"and chance to pick up a book . . . of mine!"

Although he wrote over a dozen excellent books, my father wrote more for *The New Yorker* magazine than he did in any other medium.

I have been told by many who worked with him at the magazine that my father could write rapidly on almost any topic with an elegance and vitality that made the subject shine. He turned out a constant stream of sparkling prose as a reporter for Talk of the Town, movie and theater critic, short story writer, poet, and book reviewer. Virtually every issue contained his gemlike prose; he mined for the perfect words and had an ability to link words together with an original and cheerful style that conveyed precisely what he wished to say in an amusing way. He was so happy at *The New Yorker* because his work at the magazine allowed him to write and still be in the constant flow of friends. He loved such congenial company.

"Stay with my beauty for the fire is dying," he would intone when he was at home.

My father's mother had died of a lingering cancer when he was seven. He never got over the tragedy of her long death by that disease. He liked to be surrounded by people from the time he woke early in the morning until he reluctantly spent a few hours in sleep late at night.

Probably because of his mother's slow and painful death, my father always hated the idea of ever becoming an invalid or a burden to his friends and family—he wanted to forever be a source of positive energy.

My father was like the life-giving fire, the hearth and heart of the house, continually warmed and warming those around him.

He never let the fires go out. He would pile on the logs early in the morning in our fireplace at home and keep the hearth blazing late into the night.

My father was always the first up and the last to bed. I see him now standing before the large fireplace in Bronxville or Norfolk—holding forth a glass in his hand and a large circle of family and friends standing around—laughing and delighting in his company as he, in turn, took warmth from the love he lit in our hearts.

I remember one Christmas, when I was a freshman at Yale, inviting a classmate, Lance Liebman, to spend the holidays with me. Lance was just sixteen while the rest of us were eighteen. Though younger, he was much smarter than anyone else I met in our class. He had gotten a National Merit Scholarship and arrived at Yale from Frankfurt, Kentucky. His room was across the hall from mine, and we became friends.

I knew Lance wasn't planning a trip home for Christmas, so I invited him down to spend some time with me. Lance was rather amazed by the welcoming carnival my father had created in our huge house in Bronxville. That first night there was a party of about a hundred people. Writers and publishers from New York joined neighbors and family members in a holiday celebration.

The next day my father went out and bought a twenty-foot-high Christmas tree to put in the two-story library. Christmas morning my father gave Lance a book, and my mother found another little present for him. He had become an immediate member of the Gill tribe and, as such, a participant in a constant kind of communal party.

Lance went on to become a very distinguished professor of law at Harvard, but I don't think he ever quite recovered from that experience.

Another friend of mine, Robert Goodman, an artist living in Soho, also came out for a Sunday afternoon and evening of rollicking fun.

Years later he told me: "I will never forgive you for inviting me out to your father's house. I immediately got married and had a bunch of kids. He made it look like so much fun!"

My father did, indeed, bring a playful energy to every aspect of life.

Somehow he even taught the world of philanthropy how to be more amusing.

"It is a lot more fun to spend your money while you are still alive," he informed Brooke Astor, and she followed his advice with a new zest for giving her money away. My father practiced what he preached. When he died my father had spent the fortune he inherited from *his* father, and just a little bit more money than any he ever made as a writer. We discovered that he left just enough in his bank account to pay his last American Express bill. My father had a great sense of the theater, and I am sure he could not have imagined a more perfect exit.

His lack of interest in accumulating money is also a life lesson for me in the sense that we should be as generous as we can while we are alive.

My father was just as generous with his time as he was with his money. He never failed to try to help my friends. When he met my friend William Hamilton and heard that he had been trying to get a cartoon published in *The New Yorker* since he was a student at Andover, my father became his strong advocate. I remember Jim Geraghty, who was art editor at the time, taking me aside at a party and saying: "Your father never stops badgering me about your friend Bill Hamilton. I am going to go mad!" Mr. Geraghty was smiling when he said that, but I knew there was some truth behind those words.

Another example came decades later. I was working at J. Walter Thompson when an account person, Lois Mark, told me her cousin was graduating from Harvard and what he wanted more than anything in the world was to work at *The New Yorker*. I called my father. My father not only saw the young man but he got him a job—no easy feat in those days, when *The New Yorker* was the most admired magazine in America.

I am sure Lois Mark's cousin was brilliant.

Just as I am certain today—with forty years of magnificent art to his name—that William Hamilton is a genius of social satire, our generation's Daumier.

Yet my father didn't wait for the young cousin or young William Hamilton to prove himself before; in his great generosity of spirit, he rushed forward to make their dreams come true.

In the same way he opened his arms and his world for Tina Brown when she first arrived in New York on a visit as a student at Oxford. "I knew nobody," Tina told me. We were talking on the roof of the Cosmopolitan Club where she was hosting a party—by that time she had been named editor of the magazine—to celebrate the reissue of my father's book *Here at the New Yorker*, his greatest bestseller.

"Your father took me from one famous literary person to another," Tina continued. "It was my first trip to New York. You can imagine it was one of the most exhilarating times of my life."

Tina repaid my father's generous spirit by making sure he was being published until the very last week of his life. His last piece in his beloved magazine described the power of the past to warm our hearts in the present.

His last words in the magazine where he had written for more than six decades were:

"Taking the measure of an environment that is both new and old, we begin to sense the potency of the past. In an almost literal sense, we are learning to hold out our hands to the past and feel ourselves warmed by it."

My father loved the past as much as he gave himself unstintingly to the present.

And he *always* wanted to be published. When he was just twelve years old his local paper, *The Hartford Courant*, had written an expose of some slumlords. Some of the slumlords mentioned were in his mother's family. My father immediately sat down and sent off a letter offering to give all the family real estate away. Even then his generous heart was in evidence.

The editor of the paper did not know that my father was only a young child and thought that it was an official announcement from the family. He ran my father's letter promising to give the tenants free homes on the front page under the headline "A Generous Offer."

The Duffy family, his mother's business-minded relatives, never quite forgave my father for his well-publicized giveaway, but he always loved to tell that story.

He had been published, and on the front page! Whatever dent he had made in the family fortune was well worth it!

My father loved New York City, and his delight in being in the city gave others an enhanced appreciation for the fun to be had at every opportunity—even his colleagues in what were known as the rather glum, dark hallways of the *New Yorker* offices.

Joseph Mitchell, one of my father's favorite *New Yorker* colleagues and his exact opposite as a writer and a person in almost every way—Mitchell was a shy Southerner who wrote almost nothing in the last forty years of his life compared to my father, who was a gregarious native of the Northeast and never stopped writing—once told me: "If I could bottle what your father has I could make a fortune."

My father was a handsome, even dashing man with an energetic, effervescent spirit. His desire to please and his talent in doing so was a charismatic combination.

My father loved to sing, although he never felt he had much of a voice. "Sing, Gatesy, sing," my father would encourage me when I was young. At almost every family gathering my father would like me to get to my feet and sing a few Irish songs. He believed I had a voice for song that he lacked, and he was eager to see me stand and deliver a lyrical melody.

At the end of the memorial celebration for my father I stood and led everyone in singing "Danny Boy." Although the final words are sad, the entire overflow crowd sang them with joy and gratitude:

"And I'll be there | in sunshine or in shadow | O Danny Boy I love you so!"

After the singing ended those last words reverberated for me . . . and sounded somehow like Daddy Boy.

My father never lost that sense of boyish wonder and excitement with the world he saw.

In his book about Cole Porter my father states a clear life lesson: "Those who hug life to them, though they grow older, never grow old."

My father hugged life to him with a passionate embrace that gave him the spirit of eternal youth.

In the last decades he always seemed to be in the midst of a joyous crowd. We would hug when I left a party. My father never in any real sense grew old and never lost his great zest for what each day could offer.

Even today, every day, I miss the sweet boyish pleasure he took in so many aspects of life—every building, every book, every person he encountered seemed to be full of wonder.

And I miss the creative, almost childlike joy he brought to writing and living and helping others lead a more joyous and creative life.

I would have loved to have more time to talk with my father—one on one, before he left me. I would have loved to tell my father how much I loved him—and would always love him.

Looking back now on the times we had together, I realize how much my father gave me.

As a father myself I have learned that all fathers are imperfect. I have certainly not always been the kind of father I would have liked to be. Yet I believe my children know I truly love them.

My father gave that true love to me. I never doubted for a moment that he loved me.

Now I feel sorry that he left this world before I could tell him how much he had given me.

Yet today I also feel that somehow he knows. I think he might be puzzled a bit by the joy I take in a simpler, less social life, but he would be delighted to know that I became a published writer. And he would be so pleased to be remembered in my writing as a man who gave so much. His greatest accolade when speaking of someone was to praise his or her "generosity." To him, being generous was the greatest single virtue.

As part of his generosity of spirit, my father never wanted to be a burden to anyone. When he died he wanted to go with the same forward motion he lived with: He always wanted to exit quickly—leaving a sense of love and laughter to echo down the ages.

My father left this world the way he wanted to. He felt a "back pain," made his way to a hospital, and died within hours. I think he willed himself to die once he felt he might be on the downward slide. He was probably worried he would be diagnosed with some disease that might make him incapacitated in some way. He chose to die when he was still so full of life. I think of him hurrying off the Grand Stage of his time—where he had played such an inspiring part—giving us all a quick wave of his hand and a final request: "A few more songs!" just as he would ask for late at night when we were gathered around the hearth fire at home.

At the memorial service I was left with one last chance to help him on his way . . . to sing a few more Irish songs for him. So we sang one more on his memorial day.

Afterward, we held a public celebration in Grand Central Terminal. Grand Central looked more beautiful than at any time in our lifetimes. Somehow the elaborate restoration had added an extra shine of luster to its original beauty. I looked around this wonderful space that my father, his friend Jackie Onassis, and their generous friends had saved for all of us.

Today, in the peculiar alchemy of death and departing, my father's joyous, unconquerable spirit is with me more than ever. I now see that my father had turned his childhood pain from the death of his beloved mother into a rare ability to preserve—in sparkling words and soaring stone—the best of the past for the greater good of future generations.

My father wrote, "The first rule of life is to have a good time," and he made such a happy achievement more possible for all of us with the brilliant stories and beautiful spaces he left behind.

I can see now with a new clarity *after* my father's death all the great gifts he gave to me and the larger world.

HOW THIS LESSON CAN HELP YOU

Never give up on your dreams—at any age! And remember that your dreams can be many: Just as my father loved to create great stories, he also loved to preserve the architectural creations of others. He never stopped dreaming of doing more, and he never grew too old to stop achieving great things. Our talents are not limited and should be shared with a confidence and generosity of spirit.

And since all parents are imperfect, don't judge your father too harshly, but love him as a person who brought you into life and can show you new ways to live.

And when your father dies, get ready to appreciate him more than ever and have his memory inside you as a guide and welcome source of strength.

Learn . . . From Your Mother

"Love . . . believeth all things,
hopeth all things, . . . love never faileth."
— *St. Paul's First Letter to the Corinthians*

Mother believed that life itself was a miracle and that it was full of wondrous occasions to be fully enjoyed. Mother's last day was full of miracles.

It started in the place she most loved . . . at a home called The Bungalow in the country, where she had spent the happy summers of her childhood and the passionate years of her early, married life with my father; The Bungalow was where their love had grown and expanded to love for their children and grandchildren.

This first winter after my father's death she had left the house in Bronxville and decided to brave the cold in the drafty, one-story home designed solely for summer. My mother was eagerly looking forward to a family Christmas that was to take place at The Bungalow in a matter of days. To begin her last day she took her new puppy Rodin, nicknamed Rodi, out to the lawn in the front of the house.

Mother had loved to take me out and read to me on the lawn in summer when I was a young boy. The very stones and grass and fields and trees surrounding the house conveyed so many happy memories. We could see Haystack Mountain from the lawn, which she had climbed so happily, so many times, with so many family members.

She loved the quote from the Bible "I lift mine eyes unto the hills, from whence commeth my strength." As we would ride up to the Norfolk countryside from New York, she would always exclaim, as we neared our destination, with a proud note of delighted possession, "My hills!"

Now on the last morning of her life my mother was out on the lawn of her childhood summer home, surrounded by her mountains, a sunny, memory-filled spot.

On those fields just two summers before, under a large tent, she had celebrated their sixtieth wedding anniversary, dancing with my father and many of her grandchildren.

Although the date was December 23, it was still warm. The air was fresh and dry, and the sky was sparkling. Exhilarated by the clean country air and the bright, clear winter light, Rodi bounded across the lawn and the field, toward a stone wall bordering Laurel Way. And then, being only a little puppy and unused to the dangers of the street, he leapt over the wall.

Just at that moment a truck was driving by, and the driver did not have a chance to avoid the bounding puppy racing right in front of his wheels. He ran right over the little dog.

The truck was big and heavy, and the puppy lay still at the side of the road where he had been carried by the strength of the blow from the front tires.

A car then drove by. The driver, a neighbor named Al Boucher, took in the scene of the big truck, the driver getting down from the cab, and my mother kneeling by a dying dog, and immediately drove on to Laurel Cottage, just down the road from The Bungalow, where he knew I lived.

I had planned to go into New York City that evening for a

Christmas party, but, for some reason, I had decided to cancel the trip. Al Boucher arrived at my front door.

"Your mother is with a dying dog," he said.

"What happened?" I asked.

"A truck ran over the dog. The dog looks like a goner. You had better go see your mother."

I drove up the road to see what I could do, not expecting to be able to do anything. Mother was kneeling by Rodi, the driver standing over them.

"O, Gatesy-Boy," Mother said, looking up, "I think we should take Rodi to the vet."

The driver of the paint truck looked dubious.

"I never saw him," the driver said. "He must have run out right in front of me. Can I do anything? Call anyone?"

Mother thought for a moment.

"No, let's just go to the vet. And it wasn't your fault," she said to the driver.

Mother bent down to lift Rodi, but he was too much for her. Rodi was barely breathing, almost a dead weight. I bent with the driver, and we lifted him up. Mother quickly got in the backseat of my van.

"Shouldn't we put him in a box? He's bleeding," the driver said, trying to be helpful.

"Rodi is not going in any box," my mother said in her firmest voice. "Put him on my lap."

We lifted him onto Mother's lap, his blood beginning to run down her legs. I looked at her and the dog, wondering if the trip was worthwhile. She could sense I was taking too much time in thinking.

"Let's go," Mother said, and I hurried around to the front. As I put the van in gear, I thought to myself that this was a tragic errand, sure to end badly. I could see in the rearview mirror that mother was stroking Rodi and talking to him quietly. She caught my eye.

"Talking will help him keep calm," Mother said, amazingly calm herself. "Talking can help heal him."

I did not believe that such an obviously broken body could be healed by any words, but I kept still. It seemed a very long drive to me, although it lasted less than fifteen minutes. Mother never stopped her gentle encouragement: "You'll be all right, Rodin, good dog, you'll be all right."

But by the time we neared the entrance to the vet's, Rodi was actually able to lift his head. A little. Maybe talking really did help, I thought. I hoped.

At the vet's, two women came out to help us. They had a stretcher for Rodi and helped us get him out. We carried him into the lobby, and a doctor appeared immediately.

"Is this Rodin?" he asked.

Mother almost cried at that moment—with gratitude. He remembered her dog from a previous visit! And—most important to my mother—called him by his full name!

"Yes," Mother said. "He was run over by a truck."

The doctor ran his hand over Rodi, not worrying about the blood.

"I don't feel any broken bones," he said, "but I can't be sure. And it is hard to tell about internal injuries. We will take him right in for X-rays. I will know a lot more in a few hours. Where can I call you?"

"A few . . . hours?" Mother asked.

The doctor took a look at Mother. He saw her pain and her need to know if her puppy would live or die.

"A few minutes," he said, and tears came into Mother's eyes again as she realized how perceptive the doctor had been and how responsive to her need.

The doctor turned, with Rodi, heading toward the clinic.

"Doctor," Mother said, just touching his elbow.

He stopped, waiting for Mother's instructions.

"Keep talking to him, will you? It is important to keep talking to him."

"We will," the doctor assured her.

I guided Mother over to a chair in the lobby. Two women came out and gave us each a welcome glass of cold water. The doctor came back—almost too soon, I thought.

Mother stood up, rising slowly. She was always very brave about such things, but this was going to be tough and, despite hoping against hope for the best, I could see that she was ready to hear the worst.

"He will live," the doctor said.

Now Mother did cry, just a quick tear or two, wiping them quickly away with a little handkerchief she had. I knew then that she had never really thought that Rodi would make it—despite all her encouraging talk.

"Thank you, Doctor," Mother said. "Thank you."

She held his hand.

"Well," the doctor continued, "there is still plenty to do. But no bones are broken as far as we can tell. We should keep him overnight—at least—to make sure about everything."

"Yes, yes," Mother said, relieved that her puppy was not dead at that moment and knowing now that he would somehow live. "Yes."

"And," the doctor continued, "he might turn out to be lame . . ."

"Yes," Mother said. "All right. Keep him. And keep talking to him." She was almost cheerful as she gave him that last instruction.

We turned to go. As we drove away, Mother touched my arm.

"Stop," she said. "Please. I forgot to thank those ladies for their help and for the water."

"We can do that some other time. We will be coming back," I protested.

"Now," Mother said firmly.

I turned around. Mother got out and thanked the women for the cool water they had brought us. Then we began the drive back to Norfolk again. I could sense that Mother was elated.

"That doctor has a healing touch. And he could look you in the eye and tell you."

She paused—but just for a moment.

"Rodin is a miracle dog," she said. "Did you see that truck?"

"Yes, he certainly is a strong dog to survive that encounter."

"A miracle dog," Mother insisted, overriding any lesser description, "in a time of miracles.

"Do you know," she continued, "that I am going to a Christmas concert at the church tonight, and then afterward Kate [my niece] and Laura [my daughter] are coming to stay . . . with me at The Bungalow?"

"No," I said, unaware of the arrangement.

"These are my hills," Mother said, pointing to the hills on the right as we approached Norfolk.

We drove into the driveway of The Bungalow.

"I think you should have a cup of tea," I said.

"A wonderful idea," Mother agreed.

We went in the back door, entering the kitchen.

"Now where is all that tea you gave me?"

"There," I said, pointing.

"I'll just put on some hot water."

"I think I will head off," I said.

"Oh," Mother said, "all right."

We left the water boiling in the kitchen, for Mother would

never let anyone see themselves out of The Bungalow without her at their side.

I opened the door.

"Goodbye, Gatesy-Boy." She reached up and pulled my head down toward her.

I noticed how small and frail she had become in her last years. Yet she was still powerful enough to pull my head down to her, even as I tried to pull away. She gave me a small bite on my ear. I opened the front door of The Bungalow and started out across the lawn toward the van.

Mother followed me.

"I was glad you were there, Gatesy-Boy." She came up to me and gave me another hug and a kiss.

I went out and got into the car.

She waited until I rolled down the window.

"I will call the vet's tomorrow," I said.

Her face dropped.

"Tomorrow?"

"Okay, I will call him later this afternoon."

"Good, good."

She reached into the car, grabbed my neck, and gave me another hug and a kiss.

I put the car in gear and headed down the drive.

She walked beside it.

As the car picked up speed, she ran a few steps, raised one hand, and then both hands in a great wave.

"Ooh, aahh, oooh, aahh," she called out in her musical version of the noisy family farewell.

Later that afternoon I called the vet's. "Rodin is doing fine," the doctor said. "All his vital signs are good. The bleeding has stopped. Most of the wounds look superficial. But we should keep him for at least another day. And—he may not walk quite properly again. It is hard to tell in these cases, but his body has been through a terrible trauma."

"Yes, thanks," I said. I had heard enough.

I called Mother. I knew she would be waiting for my call.

She answered on the first ring, unusual for Mother.

"Rodi is fine," I said, "but they want to keep him for another day or two."

"Wonderful," Mother said. "Such a miracle dog."

It was clear that she did not want or need any more details. She had been assured that her beloved dog would live, and that was miracle enough for Mother.

"Love you," I said, which was my usual sign-off on a phone call with Mother.

"Love you, Gatesy-Boy," she replied, which was her usual sign-off—no matter how old I had gotten.

That night it seemed that I had barely gotten to sleep when the phone rang.

I waited for the answering machine to tell me who could be calling.

It was my daughter, Laura.

"Dad, Dad, pick up, pick up."

"Laura?"

"Dad, Granmere is asleep, and she won't wake up."

"Where is she?"

"In her car."

"In her car?"

"In the driveway. And she won't wake."

"I will be right up."

I pulled on some jeans and hurried out. There was a full moon. I learned later that the moon was closer to the Earth that night than it would be again for hundreds of years. It was one of the brightest moons of the millennium. As I went up to The Bungalow, I noticed that everything was bathed in an unearthly, yet powerful light. There was a holy clarity about the night. You could see the stone walls and every needle in the pine trees.

It was easy to see Mother in her car under the blazing moonlight. The engine was running, and when I opened the door I knew immediately that she had died and yet for some reason I gave thanks that her little heater had kept going—it was still warm inside the car.

Mother had been diagnosed two years before with an aneurysm that was on an artery leading to her heart. The doctor had made the mistake of telling her that operating would be difficult and she might need a year to fully recover.

"But I don't have a year to take off!"

"Without an operation you could die at any time," the doctor had told her.

"Perfect!" Mother had said. She was not afraid of death, but she didn't want to miss a moment of life.

Mother was wearing a spectacular hat—like something the Three Kings could have worn to visit Baby Jesus. She had her favorite coat on, and her favorite earrings and necklaces.

She wore her favorite red gloves. Each year, Mother would ask me to buy her a new pair of red gloves "for special occasions." Of course, in Mother's life, there were so many special occasions. Like a Christmas concert, and having her grandchildren spend the night afterward with her at The Bungalow. She wore out at least one pair of red gloves a year.

As Mother grew older and more diminutive, she seemed to add more hats and bright clothes and sparkling jewelry to her costumes. In that bright moonlight, she looked like a great Egyptian queen, riding a lighted barge toward glory. And she was smiling. A little, proud, truly happy smile. She had been ready. She was beautifully dressed for what Henry James once called "the last, great adventure."

I took my mother in my arms as she had taken me so many

times since I was born. She had born me up, loved me, and rocked me to sleep singing softly as I lay, a small boy, safe in her arms. I gave her a kiss. She looked so beautiful. She always looked beautiful, but never more than under that moonlight.

She died as she had lived: full of high expectations heading toward another "special occasion," happy in the thought that she would be hearing some wonderful music and spending the night with her beloved grandchildren.

It has been almost ten years now since my mother died.

Mother loved life so and embraced each moment as a "special occasion." Her spirit is a great gift to me that fills and inspires me.

Mother would always start every meal with a hymn: "Praise God from whom all blessings flow/ Praise Him all creatures here below," and she would insist we *all* sing—holding hands around the dining room table.

Mother never stopped praising God or being grateful and loving to all "creatures" here below.

HOW THIS LESSON CAN HELP YOU

Remember that a mother's hopeful, never-failing love for you is one of the greatest gifts you are given. Pass it on the best you can.

Mother always took the time—even on her last afternoon—to express her thanks and gratitude to other people.

I have never forgotten how she insisted we return to thank those two ladies at the vet's before we drove back home.

Mother never let the pressure of time interfere with living as she wanted to.

Lose . . . Your Watch
(and Cell Phone and PDA)!

"No time to say hello, good-bye,
I'm late, I'm late, I'm late!"
—*The harried White Rabbit in*
Lewis Carroll's Alice in Wonderland

 Last night, when talking to a group at a bookstore, I pulled up my sleeve and exposed my naked wrist.

"Lose your watch!" I exclaimed.

Everyone's head jerked up at my powerful shout, and a few people guiltily stopped looking at their wrists or checking their BlackBerrys.

I was once like those guilty watch watchers. I constantly checked my watch—in the office or at home. With colleagues at work and even friends and family during birthday celebrations I would secretly glance at my watch, fearful that I would be late for . . . whatever!

I think in America today we have sadly perverted the Puritan Ethic we inherited. My mother's father, a direct descendent of the Pilgrims who arrived on the *Mayflower*, would tell me stories of Sundays when he was growing up in the 1890s in Calais, Maine.

"We would not be allowed to do *anything* all day. No work. No play. We had to sit quietly and think about God. That was hard for me when I was a boy."

Perhaps those strict Sundays were an unbalanced version of what was healthy for most humans. It was probably very hard for my grandfather to do nothing all day, especially as a child. But I think we have reached an equally unbalanced version of life today—always so busy filling up every second of our days with activities.

I feel concerned for those children today who spend Sundays—and every day—so scheduled with activities that they hardly get a chance to pause and think straight about God or *anything*!

And what about their overscheduled parents? In my previous life I spent my twelve-hour workdays always checking to make sure I got as much done as I could, as though racing a kind of personal achievement clock.

Today, with technology allowing us to be instantly connected to our work lives 24/7, many of us literally *never* stop working.

Checking a PDA for e-mails from colleagues and surfing the Web for the latest news have become constant tics for many people.

My brain-tumor diagnosis was a wake-up call from that kind of madness. It is a powerful reminder that our time on Earth is severely limited. We humans live much longer lives than most bumblebees but much shorter ones than most redwood trees.

To me that means that instead of scheduling every moment, we should occasionally make time to contemplate life and experience the joy that can only be found when you interrupt constant *doing* and start simply *being*.

Today I wake up, crawl out of bed (at sixty-eight, few people leap out of bed), and walk over to help "open" at my Starbucks store, where I am still a barista. By 5:30 A.M. we have to be sure that the coffee is ready, the pastries are out, the music is on, and that we are ready to greet the eager first Guests with a confident smile and serve them well. In that early-morning shift there is not a minute to waste. Yet by noon or one P.M., I am free to go out and enjoy the rest of the day.

I can go for a walk. I can spend time with my children. I can spend time by myself. I can contemplate. I can read. I can write. I can use my "free time" spontaneously, in any way I please. I can develop in any way I please. What a gift such unscheduled time is to me! My part-time job has given me a full-time life.

I don't think I would have been able to truly appreciate the new happiness I have found without this gift of time. What is sad, though, is that most of us have the choice of having *some* free time; we simply don't make it for ourselves. So many of us today are—like me in my former advertising life—living unbalanced lives and struggling to make every second count in a way that actually deprives every moment of its chance to develop.

There is a story that Buddha said his happiest moment was when he was four years old and his nurse left him alone for a few minutes. Left unattended he had a rare chance to watch a butterfly dance toward a flower and simply enjoy the light of the sun slanting through the green trees. Buddha was said to have believed that it was the first time he was left alone with unscheduled activities and had a moment of pure being—at one with the universe—that brought him a kind of spontaneous ecstasy.

With his nurse away he was able to truly experience the moment. Buddha was said to believe that such spontaneous moments were the greatest gift in this earthly life. How many peaceful, unplanned moments do we grant ourselves in our modern rush to get somewhere and do something?

Most statues of Buddha show him sitting. Is that because you can't *run* toward such peaceful epiphanies?

Perhaps these moments can only be truly experienced when you take off your watch, turn off your phone and e-mail, lose your sense of time, and let yourself be still. Don't we all feel sometimes like we are racing the clock—as though life were a sprint in which we wanted to cross the finish line first? And we are all so proud of what we are *doing*.

Do you notice in America when we meet someone new we almost always ask them: "What you do you *do*?" As though doing were more important than *being*.

We define people by what they *do* rather than who they really *are*.

Buddha would be horrified!

All our focus is on doing rather than experiencing each moment in a more profound and contemplative way. But it sure is hard to contemplate anything when we are so surrounded by the relentless counting of clocks—on our wrists, cell phones, computers, wall clocks, even gym clocks.

Thousands of years ago our ancestors paced themselves by the light of dawn creeping over the hill and the shadows of dusk falling out from the trees.

Then came church bells that rang the *hours* to keep towns on time. A farmer out in a distant field might be in touch with the hours of the day.

Next grandfather clocks were invented, becoming dominant family possessions that took the place of honor in the home—proudly ticking with great solemnity and ringing the chimes loudly on every *quarter* hour. Laurence Sterne wrote a great comic novel called *Tristram Shandy* in which the narrator's anxious concern with winding a grandfather clock has ruined his life. By the time this book was published in the eighteenth century, people realized the pernicious influence an obsession with time could have on love and life. Sterne's book featured a grandfather clock as a destructive force on family life, and it became a bestseller.

About one hundred years ago the gold *pocket* watch became a kind of symbol of success. It was given to loyal employees at their retirement to remind them of all the hard years they had worked in an office. They could take it out and glance with respect at the face as the *minutes* of what was left of their lives ticked down.

Then the *wrist*watch was invented, and it became cheap and so accessible that soon everyone was wearing one. No one left home without affixing such a timepiece to their skin. Eventually dates and time zones and latitude and longitude were displayed and watched as well, and you could go swimming or take a bath or shower without having to take your wristwatch off.

Today, with cell phones, computers, and other entrancing electronic devices, we are *never* away from the dictatorial focus on constant measures of time.

You can't return a call or take a photo without seeing precisely what time it is. In many ways we have become mental and emotional slaves to the constant, finite calculations, and it is hard to resist such an anxious focus on every ticking second.

It is hard to escape our time-centered culture. I remember with guilt an occasion during my former life as a "big shot" advertising guy when my daughter Bis grew furious with me.

Bis was in her early twenties, just beginning her career making movies in New York, and I invited her to a fancy party. I greeted her as she came in but spent much of the evening entertaining my many other illustrious guests.

"Pop," she told me, "I am very upset."

"Why?" I said. "I thought it was a great party."

"The party was okay," she said. "But I want more time with you. One-on-one time with you."

Bis was right that night. I see now that one-on-one time with your children or your family or others you love or even *yourself* is by far the most important time. Yet in our rush through life we often forget to grant ourselves that precious time and attention.

I have come to hate the expression "killing time." If you ever say to anyone "I was just killing time," catch yourself. Let time *live*.

Don't be a "clock watcher."

Arthur Ross, who became a great philanthropist and lived into his late nineties, once told me: "Don't cheat yourself of life."

He told me: "Many young people get up and tell themselves they have no time to go for a walk through the beautiful pine trees in Central Park (which Arthur had made possible). Others tell me they have no time to read or go to a museum (many of which Arthur generously funded). Yet they all have time to rush to the office and watch Wall Street prices rise or fall on their computer screens for hours on end. They all find time to answer every crazy e-mail!

"When I was a boy," Arthur continued, "there were not so many electronic addictions. I tell every young person today: Don't cheat yourself . . . give yourself time to get out and enjoy your life!"

Follow Arthur's advice: Give yourself time to fully enjoy the gift of today.

Even for just a few minutes a day. Slaves to your computers and cell phones: Throw off your electronic chains.

Free yourself!

Start with the liberating first step: Lose your watch!

HOW THIS LESSON CAN HELP YOU

Start right away by granting yourself at least one or two unscheduled hours a day. See what magic this spontaneous time can bring!

Let Go . . . And Let God

"When the hounds of spring are on winter's traces . . ."
  —*Algernon Charles Swinburne*

 Last spring I gave a talk in North Carolina. Afterward a friend took me out to the more rustic area of the Blue Ridge Mountains. He introduced me to his aunt Hattie. She is ninety-three years old and still lives in a real log cabin.

When we arrived, Aunt Hattie showed us around her farm. There were chickens roosting in the trees and a very fat pig rooting in the yard. She pushed a "stubborn" mule that was eating the first sprouts of green away from her garden patch.

Aunt Hattie seemed so relaxed in the midst of what seemed to me an unsettling, all-too-real slice of natural chaos. As we were walking and Aunt Hattie was talking, a chilly wind blew. I pulled my jacket closer around me, although I noticed Aunt Hattie seemed content to let the wind blow her white hair about. She was dressed in a long blue dress that reached down to her ankles but hardly seemed enough protection from this cold.

"I thought it was supposed to be warmer down south," I commented through clenched teeth. "I think it is nicer up in New York right now."

Aunt Hattie gave me a sharp look from her bright blue eyes.

"It's cold for this time of year . . . but you can't rush the seasons."

She paused, still looking hard at me as though I were a recalcitrant mule on her farm.

"Some city people don't understand," she told me. "Out here in the mountains, we know you just got to let go and let God."

I got her point. Most of my life I have lived in a city full of man-made structures, dependent on modern achievements like electricity for heat in the winter and air-conditioning in the summer.

There's always been a sense with me that humans are capable of conquering every natural situation, and I have tried to control many things that come my way.

I have moved quickly through many natural events—from my children's births to my advancing age. I remember when my daughter Laura was born and I took the day off to be present at her birth.

"How could you do that?" my boss at JWT asked me angrily. "We had one of the most important presentations ever going on. We needed you here."

"I know, but this is a once-in-a-lifetime—"

"It was a once-in-a-lifetime new business pitch," my boss interrupted me. "Now we'll never get the account!"

He was angry for months—maybe for years—that I had put my "personal life" ahead of my professional obligations. The corporation is a beast that is never satisfied—it always wants more from you. Until the time that it doesn't want any more and regurgitates you back to the world.

I cannot claim to be an innocent victim. I got caught up in the corporate life, where there are no seasons, only one mad dash from one "opportunity" to another. I have often been impatient with the seasons of my life, rather than experiencing them in a respectful way for what they were. I've forced many relationships rather than letting them unfold and develop naturally. Now I realize that many of the most important things in life are like the weather; we can choose to accept them with joy or hate them with a passion, but we simply cannot control them.

Aunt Hattie's words brought this life lesson home to me. I should have known those beautiful mountains could teach me things.

I had visited my mother's father one summer before I went to Yale and learned a thing or two from him as well. He had moved down to Asheville, North Carolina, during the Great Depression. It was a geographical as well as financial "comedown" for him. His great-grandfather, Solomon Gates, had moved up to Maine in 1800 when it was a wilderness and still part of the state of Massachusetts. He started a lumber business in the virgin forests there. His son, Ephraim Church Gates, expanded the business by sending schooners full of lumber down to Boston and New York. And *his* son, Church Ephraim Gates, after fighting with his Maine regiment in the Civil War, decided to open retail lumberyards in New York City. The business boomed as the city grew.

My grandfather, whom I called Grampro, had led an easy life as heir to this lumber empire. When he was a little boy, his mother would take him to Egypt to avoid the long New England winters. He went to Hotchkiss and Yale. He fell in love and got married and had children and never worried about money. Then things seemed to change overnight.

"When the Depression happened," Grampro told me over breakfast that summer I spent with him, "everything stopped cold. No one built another house."

Grampro had gone down to Asheville to run a very small business a relative had found for him. Grampro and a few other helpers delivered coal and beer around town. Grampro gave me a job that summer helping out.

We would get up every morning at five A.M., and Grampro would make us each one soft-boiled egg and a cup of coffee. I was only eighteen but already a know-it-all.

"I have heard that too many eggs and too much coffee is not good for you," I told him after a week or so of the exact same breakfast.

He looked at me out of his clear blue eyes. Grampro was a handsome man. He sat straight even at the breakfast table. He had grown up in the horse-and-carriage era and seemed to sit with a straight back even when eating at the breakfast table, as though he were still riding a horse.

Once Grampro had taken me out for a ride. He wanted to share his love for horses with me. We went out on some horses he had borrowed from a friend in his neighborhood of Biltmore Forest, a little village just outside Asheville. It was a place much like Norfolk, high up in the hills and very rustic. There were many horse trails winding through the forest.

Grampro trotted ahead with perfect posture on his horse. Within minutes my horse could sense I was a poor rider and headed for home. I could do nothing but cling to the bridle as my horse raced back to the stable. Grampro turned his horse around and caught up with me just as I was dismounting.

"Don't worry," he said, "the main thing is your horse got some good exercise!"

Now here I was, a man so full of my new nutritional wisdom and attempting to tell my grandfather what to eat.

"I think," he said slowly, giving me that unblinking look of his, "that after eighty years I will continue to have my egg and coffee."

We didn't discuss it again. Despite his old-fashioned courtesy, Grampro was quite a tough nut. He seemed very slight and thin, but I had seen him lift cases of beer as though they were feathers and toss them into a truck.

He also had courage you could feel. The mountain men working for him all grew to respect and have affection for him. Grampro spent hours trying to teach them how to read—or at least to sign their name. They were men of a time and a place where many had not completed school.

An Old Testament sense of justice was in those hills where I would go out to deliver coal or beer. A man I was working with one day told me: "I'm going to take tomorrow off."

This was rare in those days, for everyone needed every dollar they could earn. The Great Depression had not left these old mountains yet—even in the 1950s, when I was working there.

"Why?" I asked, although I had been told never to ask questions.

Willard Rice, a big mountain man my grandfather had assigned to look after me when on deliveries, told me: "Never speak until they say hello." Willard was smiling as he told me this, but I was listening carefully because he hardly ever said anything. "They don't like Yankees and they don't like strangers down here. And *never* ask any questions."

I figured out later that this was because of the history of making moonshine in the mountains, and the stills had to be kept secret. But I had to ask Jameshenry (everyone called him by the two names) why he was taking the day off.

"I told your grandfather I had some personal business."

Any sane person would have left it at that. But I was young and pushy.

"What does that mean?"

Jameshenry stopped shoveling coal. He had tried to teach me how to lift the shovel with your back rather than your arms. I was a slow learner and could never lift the tons of coal he could in a day.

"Two weekends ago," Jameshenry said, pausing a moment to

lean on his shovel, "a man at a funeral pushed my pregnant wife. Into a grave. I'm going to kill him."

I shut up after that. Almost every morning I would overhear Willard and the other men talking about someone who had "knifed" someone else or something similar. Fights ended in deaths in these hills. I learned later that these mountains produced some of the greatest Marines.

Grampro, although a Yankee, was accepted by these men, maybe because he was from the same kind of Old Testament stock. There was no bend in him.

"Once a man stuck a gun in my face," he told me during one of our breakfasts. "I was just your age, coming home from the lumberyard in New York, where I had spent the week helping out my father. I just had a bag with my dirty laundry in it, but this crook thought it was the payroll for the whole company I was carrying. I wasn't about to be pushed around like that. I swung the bag at him. He shot me in the face."

"What happened?" I asked.

"I'm still here, aren't I?"

I learned later that the bullet had gone in one side of his mouth, knocked out a few teeth, and exited from the other side. Grampro was not only brave but also very, very lucky to be alive. But not that lucky in some other dimensions of life.

After the family's lumber operation collapsed, the new business in Asheville had sounded good to my grandfather. It was an operation delivering coal to heat homes in winter and beer to drink in summer, and it sounded like a business that couldn't fail. But then people began switching from coal to oil. And the beer he was distributing was Blatz Beer, which went out of business after several years of trying to compete with Budweiser.

So Grampro, through no real fault of his own, struggled all his life to make a living. Yet I never heard him complain.

I can see him now at that little breakfast table, throwing back his head and letting out a great, booming laugh.

"Live every day of your life," Grampro wrote me in a postcard when I got back home up North.

I kept that postcard, and those words echoed in my mind. Just like Aunt Hattie's reminder to let go and let God. Grampro, like Aunt Hattie, didn't shake his fist against the universe or complain of an unkind fate.

Heading back to New York in the plane that night after visiting Aunt Hattie, I started to sing a song. I had no idea where it came from then, and I still don't. So let's just say this song was born in the Blue Ridge Mountains of North Carolina.

Here's the song that I sang and wrote down as the plane headed back up North after I heard Aunt Hattie's wise words:

Let Go and Let God
No man can force the sun to shine
Let go and let God
Spring will come in its good time
Let go and Let God
Don't try to dictate your fate
Let go and Let God
Watch, live, and create
Let go and Let God
Travel where the saints have trod
Let go and Let God
Spare your critical, judgment rod
Let go and Let God
Be the best that you can be
Let go and Let God
Then accept life's mystery
Let go and Let God

HOW THIS LESSON CAN HELP YOU

Your life is like the weather: You can talk about it a lot, but in the most profound way, you can never completely control it. Do the best you can, and then let go and let God.

Laugh . . . With New Insight

"Laughter is the best medicine."

—*Proverb*

 Being fired from a job and having a new son unexpectedly when I was fifty-seven turned out to be unexpected blessings. Although both of these events were shocks that seemed to upend my world, they were both great gifts in their own way. Unemployed, I was able to spend time with my son when he was too young even to crawl. It was a joy to see him at that age, when I could throw a little stuffed moose up toward the ceiling, and he would laugh with delight.

Before Jonathan's birth, I was in a downward spiral of depression and sadness. I had forgotten how to laugh at myself and laugh with surprise and laugh even at the simplest sights: the wind taking a leaf and tossing it in the air, the sudden rain shower that drenches us unexpectedly—those hundreds of moments during every day when, if we give ourselves a chance to truly experience them, *we can laugh with life*. Laughing with life—rather than taking everything that happens so seriously—is a prescription for a kind of healthy mental and emotional happiness that I had forgotten.

I recovered the spontaneous joy of living in the moment when

I was given a chance to spend time with my newborn child. He was so new to life, he was not afraid to laugh with uninhibited glee at me and every other thing he would see.

When Jonathan came into my life, he gave me that key insight: Life can be *funny*. It was funny to him when I made a face, scrunching up my lips and closing my eyes, and then popping them open again suddenly. It was funny to him when I stumbled carrying his cereal toward him and a bit fell on the floor. I learned to laugh with him—at myself and at all the tiny surprises of life.

In medieval times every king would have his joker—to make fun of him and remind him that he was simply human. Today we have late-night television comics who make sense of the world by reminding us of how much serious nonsense is talked about in the daylight hours.

Laughter is essential for adding a healthy perspective and puncturing pompous people who claim to control the world.

In my personal and professional failures I had somehow forgotten how to truly laugh.

I don't mean simply to laugh at a particular joke, but to laugh *without fear and with a relaxed attitude toward your fate when you are upended by life*—to see its various turnings and frequent chaos as a kind of chance to simply relax, smile, and laugh at my pathetic pretence of control. Life is full of opportunities for us to slip on the proverbial banana peel. We have a choice to treat such an unexpected fall as a tragedy or a comedy. It is probably better for our health to laugh as we slide along life's slippery pavement.

From Charlie Chaplin to Tina Fey—they help us see the absurdity of trying too hard to control life, and we are helped when we can add such understanding and laughter to our day.

Jonathan, like most newborn children, could laugh and delight in life. Jonathan's natural instinct to greet the wonder of life with laughter helped me to move forward emotionally and let me put down my burden of taking life so seriously.

Jonathan would gurgle and smile as I touched his little chest. He would grasp my fingers in his hands, look into my eyes, and transfer to my heart his great love of life. There were no walls between Jonathan and me. There were no walls between Jonathan and life itself, no carefully built defenses.

Sharing his earliest moments gave me the sense of how rare and full of wonder every moment can be. How easily most of us become jaded as we grow older. At any age, we can all learn to open our eyes again, simply from spending time with the *youngest* among us.

Since I didn't have to rush to an office, I got to see Jonathan early almost every morning. I am a morning person and love to get up at four or five A.M. Jonathan's mother was happy to have another hour or two of sleep. Jonathan woke up early like I did. I would go over to his mother's house and take him from his mother's arms so that she could get a little extra rest.

In those early hours of his life, Jonathan and I would watch the sun come up. Slowly. It would take an hour or two as the sky gently lightened—the dark subtly replaced by a lighter and lighter blue, and then the first rays of sun just peeking out. It was like seeing life with new sight.

As I watched the early light with Jonathan, I realized more fully than ever that every day is born new. Sometimes I'd feed him a bottle, rocking in a chair. His big blue eyes never left my face. His delicate little fingers would occasionally leave the bottle itself to explore my jaw or touch my eyebrow. Everything was new to him and new to me again. Sometimes I would sing to him softly, and he would smile and raise a little hand as though conducting along with the melody.

Once he learned to crawl, we would crawl together along the

living room rug to the couch. I would help him scramble up and sit him toward the back of the couch. I would stay on the floor and toss a stuffed giraffe up to him, and he would laugh and toss it back to me.

So many simple acts brought a smile or a laugh to his lips. If I looked away and then looked back at him very quickly, he would laugh. If I scrunched up my face, he would laugh. His laugh had the tuneful music of the purest kind of tiny bell.

As Jonathan got older and learned to walk and then run on his little chubby legs, we developed new games. I would hold him tight and then he would pull away from my arms and run with all his might. He was so proud of his new ability. Getting to the end of the room, he would turn and laugh. I would laugh back.

"What a fast runner you are," I would say.

He would run back to me, and I would hug him and embrace him, then he would start to struggle to get away. He wanted to run again. Hundreds of times. One morning, pulling out of my arms as I pretended to try and not let him go, Jonathan discovered he could run backward. He stumbled a few steps back and then moved his little feet faster. He stopped just before the far couch. He laughed with joy! He ran forward to me and backward from me all that early morning, laughing with glee at his new accomplishment.

I loved those laughing times with Jonathan, watching him delight in his new physical abilities.

But sometimes we would just sit together quietly in a kind of brief break and watch the wind in the distant trees. He might point with a small finger as the branches turned and shook.

"Tree," I would say.

He would make a sound like "tree" in return.

A counterpoint of discovery. He would smile and laugh with me as we named the world together. Even the act of exchanging words brought a burbling spring of happy laughter to his lips.

Later in the morning his mother would come into the living room, rubbing the sleep out of her eyes.

Jonathan would laugh with delight when he saw her and his whole body would squirm with excitement.

Despite the time he'd had with me, Jonathan had missed his mother. And despite her need for refreshing sleep, his mother had missed Jonathan. His little arms reached out for her as she lifted him back into her embrace.

Loving and laughing, they were clearly so happy to be together again after just a few hours apart.

Laughter, especially when shared with someone else, can be the best way to regain a healthy mental and emotional perspective.

It is also a lot more fun to laugh with life than to try to control every moment of every day!

HOW THIS LESSON CAN HELP YOU

Laughter is a gift of mental health we can grant ourselves at any time in our lives, but it is especially important to laugh when things are not going the way we imagined they would.

Jonathan's natural ability to laugh at life with pure joy and lack of fear taught me an important lesson: that it is crucial not to let serious concerns keep you from experiencing the miracle of every unfolding moment.

Another lesson I learned from my time with Jonathan is that sometimes when your life dramatically changes, it gives you a chance to discover new gifts you would never otherwise have received from those newly born to life.

When you get such a chance, spend as much time with the young as you can. Their delight in life is a reminder of the wonder we can all feel. At every age!

I never would have learned that lesson if I hadn't been fired from the job that had me working twelve-hour days in my past life.

When my other children were born, I didn't get to spend that kind of precious time with them one-on-one because I was rushing to work.

Today I am so grateful that I was fired in time to have those mornings with Jonathan.

The laughter we shared will always sound as a cheerful reminder: Delight in life!

LESSON 12

Live . . . Each Day with Gratitude
Like It Might Be Your Last

"You work and work for years and years, you're always on the go
You never take a minute off,
Too busy makin' dough
Enjoy yourself, it's later than you think
Enjoy yourself, while you're still in the pink
The years go by, as quickly as a wink
Enjoy yourself, enjoy yourself,
It's later than you think!"

—song from the Great Depression

Sometimes it takes a health scare to make you appreciate your life. At least that is what happened to me.

At sixty-three I went to see a doctor for a "routine" physical. That was a mistake. After sixty there is no such thing: They are bound to find *something* wrong with you!

Like most people, I avoided doctors. Doctors were for sick people, and I didn't feel sick. I just had this ringing in my ear, which was annoying and sometimes made it hard for me to sleep, so I decided to see somebody. The doctor came highly recommended.

My doctor examined me and then recommended a "routine"

MRI to take a look inside my brain. I did not know then what I know today: There is no such thing as a "routine" MRI when it comes to the brain.

When I returned to his office the doctor moved toward me with my MRI photo and he was smiling. He told me with barely contained excitement that I had a "rare form of brain tumor" but that he was a brain surgeon, he had written articles on just my kind of tumor, and he could operate tomorrow!

He actually started looking around his desk to see if he could find an article he had written on my condition.

Meanwhile, I stood frozen in fear at the mortal shock I had been given.

He turned and said that although it was a serious operation, "most people survive." Yet he had just told me how "rare" I was!

He also said I would probably lose the hearing in my left ear—even if the operation to remove the tumor was successful. He was so clearly eager to operate immediately. I told him I had no health insurance. Like many people fired from corporate life, I had let my insurance lapse. We decided to wait.

Today I am still doing what I call "watchful waiting" and what my doctor would probably call procrastination. On my last visit with him, he told me that "it is easier to take it out when it is small" and there would be fewer complications. He still wanted to open my skull and put me under the knife.

Michael J. Fox came into my Starbucks store the other day. He was there to talk with me in preparation for a television special he was doing about optimism and happiness. Michael said that he had almost the exact same unnerving kind of experience when he was diagnosed with Parkinson's disease.

"My doctor was so excited," Michael told me. "He said: 'You have Parkinson's. But it is *good news* because we got it at an early stage and I am sure they will have a cure before it goes too far.'"

Michael shook his head.

"Doctors are so in love with their diseases!"

"Too much in love," I said. "They seem to love the disease more than their patient!"

I know that my reaction is not completely rational, but my doctor's enthusiasm to operate has made me ever less enthusiastic about the prospect.

I hasten to add that my tumor is not cancerous. If it had been then I am sure I would move forward and let my enthusiastic doctor open my head.

Or *almost* sure. I am so in love with my life today, I hate to even contemplate leaving it. And I certainly have no desire to leave my little life hooked up to machines in some huge hospital in the city.

If I go—or maybe at this stage of my life it is fair to accept with grace my approaching end and simply state "*when* I go"—I would much prefer to die surrounded by the trees or under a blue sky.

I have finally made plans and drawn up a will. I have told my children I want to be buried in the woods in the country by the side of a path I used to clear in the summers. I want to be buried next to where we buried one of Mother's favorite dogs. I would literally be "going to the dogs."

And I have always loved the idea that dog spelled backward is "God." I have known so many dogs that seem to me to live a higher form of life. They are so loving and so willing to match your every mood: eager to play or simply sit quietly by the fire if you need a more contemplative time. Dogs raise their eyes to us with such a clear sense of connection. I like the idea of going back to the dog my mother loved and back to the land I loved.

Several months ago an organization called the Brain Tumor Foundation asked me to do a ribbon cutting for them. They had worked hard to raise money from private donors and the City of New York to have a mobile unit to test for brain tumors. The ribbon cutting was to help publicize that unit.

Brain tumors are often not caught until the very end, when someone falls over or has other severe problems. Most brain tumors become fatal pretty quickly, so it is still best to catch them as early as you can.

They had another brain-tumor patient ready to cut the ribbon for the big occasion, but he had died unexpectedly. I was the last-minute replacement. Despite my fear of the whole subject and the rather scary invitation that was only given because the other brain-tumor person had died earlier than prophesied, I decided I *should* go.

It was hard to admit to myself that I even had a brain tumor, let alone that I could become a kind of poster boy for that frightening condition.

At the ribbon-cutting ceremony I met another doctor. I asked him later about something I had heard of recently: the Gamma Knife. This was a treatment to target a tumor with radiation. In my eagerness to avoid surgery, I found that such a process held the hope that I might not have to go under a real, old-fashioned knife.

"Unfortunately," the doctor told me, "while it seemed like the Gamma Knife procedure was very efficacious at first, we've had some less promising results as we've tracked the patients in the last few years."

"What do you mean?" I said, not understanding his words but catching the general drift that radiation might not be right for me.

"Well," the doctor said, "to put it bluntly: There have been cases when the tumor was apparently successfully treated with a Gamma Knife, but just a few years later, the patient began to lose balance."

"Lose balance?" This sounded serious. At my Starbucks store I was often balancing hot coffee. This would not be good for my job!

"Yes," the doctor continued. "The brain is responsible for balance, and it turns out that the radiation may upset something inside. The brain is a very delicate and complex instrument. We don't know quite why at this point, but there seem to be some severe later effects. Losing balance can be quite serious—at any age."

Here the doctor gave me a look as if to say: "Especially at your advanced age!"

I had a sudden image of myself falling down the steep little stairs to my attic apartment. Not good!

So while I am not wild about having a brain tumor, I am feeling very good about my decision to avoid having the operation. I would rather live with a ringing in my ear than no hearing at all. I would rather risk some growth of my tumor and avoid the uncertainty of a major operation.

I am going to have another MRI soon, and if the tumor hasn't grown too much, I will congratulate myself . . . I might be able to wait longer to have my skull opened! I have discovered the lesson of how *relative* everything is in life. I would never have imagined that having an MRI that showed a tumor but slow growth would be a victory for me!

"Yea!" I will joyfully exclaim.

Isn't it wonderful how human beings can adapt to things so quickly? It is also surprising how soon we can gain new and better perspective from even the worst kind of news. Although I would never in a million years have chosen to have it, I have to admit my brain tumor has made me more *grateful for every moment that I can still walk and breathe.*

Life itself has never been more precious to me. And I have

found a new peace in my sense of humility. We can't choose when and where and how we are born. And we can't choose our deaths.

I shared with Michael J. Fox, on the cup of a Starbucks coffee, the quote from Wynton Marsalis that I had used to open the first chapter of *How Starbucks Saved My Life*:

"The humble improve."

"That's right," Michael agreed. "Humility is key."

We both agreed that such a feeling and sharing such insights were some of the big, unexpected benefits of facing our own personal mortality. And it is true that I am now much more humble before my destiny—whatever it turns out to be—and as accepting as I can be with the sense of death.

Yet that is not to say that I am completely cured of my fear of death. I think there is something deep within all of us that just won't let go. We seem programmed to latch onto even the slimmest sign that we can outwit the odds and last a little longer than anyone imagined.

The other morning I woke up with a crazy idea for a song about my brain tumor. I have found singing always makes me feel better.

Here's the song I sang that morning:

Brain Tumor Blues

In America we like to win—not to lose
We like to pick . . . we like to choose
I've got the Brain Tumor Blues
Now I truly know it's true:
There's nothin' I can do
So I'll just enjoy each day
And find a way to play
I'll sing a song or two
I've got the Brain Tumor Blues

Nothin' I can do
So I'll just sing—with joy so crazy and hu...
I got the Brain Tumor Blues!

I felt much better after singing that silly...

And I have heard from many people a...

being diagnosed with much worse diseases has in a ...

freed them to forget stupid worries, forgive old wrongs, and appreciate the true glory of living much more.

I have found that truth as well. Now if there is rain, as I walk
I hold my face up, eager for every drop. Swimming in a mountain
lake in the late fall, I shiver in the wind as I get out, but that chill
makes me feel more alive. Happiness is not the absence of a sense
of our mortality but living with that reality.

Happiness is not the absence of pain but accepting the pain as
part of life that occurs at every age and every circumstance. Having five children, I know well that the labor pains are terrible. At
least to me as a cowardly male, I am still in awe of a woman's ability to go through such primal agony and still, seconds later, embrace her newborn child with such unconditional joy.

But blood and screaming is as much a part of birth for the
mother as is the scream—the shout of life—with which a baby
first greets the world outside the womb. There are few things as
sweet in the world as that newborn-baby smell when you pick up
your child and hold this precious creation close.

A baby *is* born in pain, and then is subject to teething and all
the other quite accurately called "growing pains." Every toddler
or growing child comes home from school with bumps and bruises
after an active day. Yet you don't hear children complain. They
are too excited by the new possibilities of every fresh moment.

On the other hand, I have noticed that many of my contempo-
raries begin to fill their conversations with their latest medical

me! Such complaining is an affront to the miraculous
life itself. Let us not focus on our physical "growing pains"
we grow older. Growing pains are *lifelong*—and a sign of life itself; they just change in their nature, but they are always with us.

If you feel some pain in your joints as you struggle to get out
of bed in the morning—as I often do—that means you are still
alive!

There is also a strange and powerful gift of knowing life is
short . . . of living with that powerful fact before you at all
times—it brings your mind and body more in tune with the seasons of life.

I learned the valuable lesson that life is so short and meant to
be enjoyed from two friends who have died. In some ways their
deaths reinforced the positive attitude they took toward every
moment of life. Their examples are with me daily.

Arthur Lennox and Jim Donohue both gave me the great gift
of appreciating and enjoying every second we have been given.

When I think of Arthur Lennox, I remember most vividly a
morning we shared in Vancouver. We sat in the restaurant on the
top floor of our hotel for breakfast. There were already many people busily ingesting their first meal of the day. There was a buffet
spread out and a line waiting to load up on bacon and eggs.

"Maybe we can eat outside," Arthur said. "It looks like such a
lovely day."

Arthur was right. The sun was shining brightly—a rare event
for Vancouver. We made our way out toward the sun.

Arthur had a gift for having a good time. He was our client at
J. Walter Thompson in charge of the Labatt's beer account, and he
had suggested we build a campaign for a brand called "50"—in
honor of the 50th Anniversary of the company—with a song
called "Enjoy Yourself."

Labatt's 50 had become Canada's number-one-selling beer. So

we were in a celebratory mood that morning. We walked over to the glass doors looking out on the terrace. There were some tables out there—but nary a person sitting at them. I pulled at the doors. They opened. Arthur and I walked out. We lifted our faces to the warmth of the sun.

"Almost like summer," Arthur said. "You are very lucky, Michael."

"Yes," I agreed. I had written some new scripts for the television commercials, and we had decided to shoot them in Vancouver. We wanted to picture people in beautiful surroundings and Vancouver—with the shining Pacific and the flourishing pine trees—was one of the most beautiful spots in the world. Yet it was often soaked in rain. Somehow the sun had shone late the day before, in time for our shoot, and today looked even better.

Or maybe Arthur was simply referring to the fact that I was lucky the sun was out for a second day in a normally rainy Vancouver. In any case, I did feel very lucky at that moment. Any moment with Arthur was to be savored. Having spent many years with clients who were almost always angry about something, Arthur's sunny disposition was a relief to me.

"Yes," I said again, "I am a very lucky fellow to be with you this morning."

"We should celebrate," Arthur said.

A waitress appeared.

"How are you gentlemen doing?" she said, unfazed that we had made our way out to the vacant patio.

"Couldn't be better," Arthur said, giving her a big smile.

Arthur was a good-looking fellow with white hair and blue eyes. He was rather tall and carried himself with a cheerful confidence, as though he were commanding a battalion. Arthur told me once that during the Second World War, when he was stationed in London, he had a beautiful overcoat made.

"Even though I was just a lowly lieutenant, I looked like a general," he said. "Everyone saluted me."

Arthur had the gift of making good things happen. It was no accident he had taken a tiny brand of beer and built it into Canada's favorite beverage. And it was typical that he did it with a song inviting everyone to enjoy themselves.

I had a sudden idea.

"How about some ice cream?" I said.

It did feel like summer to me, the first time since I had been in Canada that I had actually felt the warmth of the sun.

"Wonderful idea," Arthur agreed.

Arthur and I were separated by several decades. He was in his fifties; I was in my early thirties. But our spirits were aligned. He sensed—despite my disguise as a hardworking advertising guy—that I was a free spirit willing to take flight. I felt Arthur to be a rare mixture of brains and a true love for every moment of life. Most important: We shared the same sense of humor. We thought it was funny to play the fool in a gentle, whimsical way. Not too over the top. Simply doing things that others might think rather . . . *eccentric*.

We both enjoyed the idea that life could be amusing if you mixed things up a bit and didn't take yourself or what you were doing too seriously.

Arthur was a relief for me because I could be myself: a guy who really didn't know quite what he was doing. With my other clients I had to pretend that I was a serious businessperson. Arthur, from the first moment, saw through that pretense.

You know how sometimes you meet someone and there is no need for any polite conversation—you both are united in spirit from that first moment in a kind of deep understanding? That was true for Arthur and me. Despite our age difference he was like a benevolent father, a loving brother—or perhaps just a favorite playmate.

The day before I had noticed a felt hat in a store and brought it to Arthur's attention. It was a big hat of a particularly garish color of blue.

"You must have that," Arthur said.

I went in and bought the blue one for myself, a green one for Arthur, and an orange one for Adrian, who was the account man, or "suit," on Labatt's.

"Maybe we should get some for the crew," Arthur suggested.

I bought ten more hats in a rainbow of colors. (One of the great things about being with Arthur was that I could buy stuff on an expense account. Labatt's was one of the most profitable accounts at the agency, and anything under the heading of "client service" was never questioned.) That day we were all wearing brightly colored hats as we went around Vancouver with our vans and cameras.

"The Irish are born with the gift of knowing the world is mad," the playwright William Sheridan had once stated.

Arthur, a proud Scot, matched my Celtic sense that the world was mad, and it was enjoyable to play the mad hatter.

Although the Labatt's campaign was about enjoying beer with friends, after college I found that I could not drink and work. I remember throwing up the booze from the night before in a bathroom at about seven thirty in the morning at J. Walter Thompson. I realized at that instant I could not be both a workaholic and an alcoholic. Sadly, I had to choose. I chose work as my next addition. So I had given up "the drink" as the Irish say. Ice cream had become my favorite indulgence. Ice cream had replaced drink as a treat for me.

Five years later I was able to work my way onto the Labatt's account. Although I no longer drank, I maintained my affection for those drinking days gone by. I had come to Arthur's attention at the agency when I had written a memo that began with this paragraph:

"I have spent at least ten years of my early life researching beer in many countries in the world. I have drunk beer in the morning at the Oktoberfest in Munich. I have sat for hours in a Paris café drinking beer after beer as the world walked by. I have drunk beer with beautiful, funny women and ugly, funny men. I have solved all the world's problems—again and again. I have drunk beer at bullfights, prizefights, and late nights in hundreds of bars across North America. I have come to just one conclusion: *Beer tastes better when it's cold.*"

Arthur had loved that last line. He hated methodical research. He loved life too much to have it categorized and analyzed. And his instincts—no focus groups or research modules for him—to go with a song had been so successful.

"Ice cream," Arthur exclaimed that morning. "A perfect breakfast!"

Our waitress brought out a large silver bowl filled with a dozen scoops of chocolate, vanilla, strawberry, and raspberry ice cream. As the sun grew stronger Arthur and I tasted every flavor. Occasionally Arthur would ask for a song.

First I sang "The Scottish Soldier," which was one of his favorites. To sing that rollicking warrior song about death and dying, you had to march with a confident soldier's swing of the arms and slamming down of the feet in the British tradition. If you have ever seen Changing the Guard at Buckingham Palace, you get the idea. Fortunately the patio was empty and I was able to sing loudly and march without inhibition:

> *There was a soldier*
> *A Scottish soldier*
> *Who wandered far away*
> *And soldiered far away*
> *There was none bolder*

With big broad shoulder
He fought in many a fray
And fought—and won
He'd seen the glory
He'd told his story
But now he's dying
His heart is crying
For he must fade away
In a far land

(Chorus to be sung at the top of one's power)
Because those green hills
Are not Highland hills
Or the Ireland hills
They're not my land's hills
And fair as these green foreign hills may be
They are not the hills of home.

Arthur applauded.

I returned to the table thinking that it was a happy accident that I had called my Labatt's campaign "Coming Home to 50." Maybe there was some deep resonance to every person at the idea of returning home for true happiness—in life or death.

"Any other brave songs about death?" Arthur asked me with a smile.

"Yes," I replied. And sang him an old Irish song made famous by the Clancy Brothers.

Here's to the widow
Bloody great female
Isn't it grand boys
To be bloody well dead

Don't have a sniffle
Go have a bloody great cry
For the longer you live . . .
The sooner you bloody well die!

Years later I heard from Arthur's widow, Marjorie, that he had died. By that time I had been fired from J. Walter Thompson and was going through some hard times. But I wanted to make the effort to pay my last respects to Arthur. He was a man worthy of respect. Arthur was no longer a major client. I was no longer a creative director. But I flew up to Canada to celebrate Arthur's life as a grateful friend and the valuable lessons about life that he had taught me. I could see by then that he had been a good role model for combining enjoyment of life with work. Unlike me, he didn't have to be so serious and focused that he lost joy and a sense of humor about life.

Marjorie invited me to give his eulogy. I spoke of how much Arthur had meant to me and to everyone he encountered. That his gift was for enjoying life while also making sure to have his priorities right—he raised some great children and he and Marjorie, unlike some married couples, always had a good time together. He achieved great things for Labatt's—but Arthur always kept his own, rare wit and gift for sharing his love for life.

I spoke of the song for Labatt's that Arthur so loved about *enjoying* yourself—it's later than you think—and how, now, so many years later, I had realized what a wonderful truth that melody contained. I told Marjorie and Arthur's children and everyone gathered there that of all the people I had met in my life, few seemed to live with such an exuberant capacity to make the most of every minute.

Arthur was a gift to me at a time in my life when I was working so hard and taking life so seriously. The times with Arthur were like visiting another world—where play and laughter could be shared, and yet success could also be achieved.

I was lucky that day but unlucky in the sense that I only fully came to appreciate his example after he was gone. I spent decades in a world of sad focus on material things without the leavening of any true perspective.

And I was too young when I knew Arthur to really take his advice about having a good time. I took life too much for granted and always thought I could have some good times "later." I spent so much time in the office—often leaving home before my children were awake and coming back home after they were asleep. In my twenty-six years at J. Walter Thompson advertising agency, I took only three sick days.

Another friend who showed me how to appreciate every moment of life, in a very different way, was Jim Donohue. Jim also left this life before I could thank him for that lesson. I lost my friend suddenly and had no time to say good-bye.

"Jim is dead," Barbara, his wife, called to say one Sunday night.

"NO," I screamed, and then: "What happened?"

"We were up in the Adirondacks. A storm came up."

"I'll be there."

Early the next morning I arrived at their home. Barbara was alone in the kitchen. I saw Jim's hiking boots by the table.

"He was wearing those," Barbara said.

I went over to pick up Jim's boots. They were still wet and very heavy.

"We had gone up with friends. We had just finished a big picnic. Do you think it was that? Jim so loved his food, and the doctor told him to watch his diet."

A few months before Jim had been diagnosed with a possible heart problem, which he had told me about when he came up to

Norfolk. We had gone over to the lake for a dock fight, something I loved to do with my old friends. The added Sumo wrestler–like bulk I had acquired over the years gave me an advantage over men who had been serious jocks when we were at school.

When we were in high school and college Jim had been a great runner. He was always very strong. That day I stood on the edge of the dock and said: "Take your best shot."

Jim moved toward me, his large hands and strong arms trying to force me backward into the water. I gripped him, turned him, and tossed him quite easily into the lake. At first, I thought he might have let me win—although that would not be like Jim. He was quite competitive. As he pulled himself back up to the dock he said: "My doctor told me to take it easy."

"Maybe we shouldn't have done it at all."

"No, no, it's just that I shouldn't go nuts with physical exertion. He told me moderate diet and exercise would work fine. I've already lost fifteen pounds."

Jim did look well—better than ever. Looking back now, maybe it was like the Tim Russert tragedy, in which his doctor thought he was doing so great but inside his heart was clogged.

That day Jim had brought his young son Michael up to be with us. I wasn't sure if Jim had named his son Michael after me, but I was sure Jim loved me. He had sacrificed quite a lot for our friendship.

Jim's friendship was a lesson to me to be loyal to the most important things in life—*and not become involved in hatred fostered by some old religious ideologies.*

His father, Al Donohue, was a hater—an Irish Catholic who hated all Protestants, or even people who might be associated in any way with what he regarded as the English, Protestant church. Jim's father had been born poor but had won a successful job on

Wall Street. He worked with men of every religion but in his heart was still alive with anger toward the church and the people he felt had so hurt his ancestors in Ireland. He could not—despite his new, affluent reality—give up the history of hurt. His hate was his most powerful passion.

Jim, his eldest son, refused to be drawn into that ancient ideological battle—despite the fights it caused with his father. They even had a fight about Jim being my roommate at Yale since I was a Protestant.

Jim arrived at our room sweating and carrying many bags. His parents never showed.

Jim told me years later that on the drive up to New Haven, when his father heard that he had decided to room with me, he had stopped the car and forced Jim to get out with all his stuff on the Merritt Parkway—at least ten miles from the Yale campus.

He thought of me as part of the Protestant world he hated.

After Jim died, his father refused to attend the funeral because Barbara had the service in a Protestant church.

Barbara herself was a Protestant. Jim had made me his best man and I remember the rehearsal dinner and all the stress. I would sing an Irish song and then Barbara's brother would sing some English song. More than just being Protestant, Barbara's father was English. Al's worst nightmare.

But I was also the enemy because my father called himself a "collapsed Catholic" and had left the "true church" and I myself had become a Protestant. My mother was an Episcopalian and active in her church, and I followed her lead.

I was shocked that Jim's father refused to attend his service because it was in a Protestant church. We had never hated so hard in our family.

My father and grandfather had taught me that you didn't have to let hates or wrongs from the past interfere with your ability to live a happy life in the present.

My Irish-American grandfather, Michael Gill, for whom I was named, was poor and grew up in a time and a place when Irish Catholics were minorities who were discriminated against. He would have had every reason to feel hatred toward those who had oppressed him. He had a rich history of wrongs to draw upon.

Yet my grandfather Gill always seemed to have a positive disposition to the world. That is not to say that he had no memory of his unfortunate history. He wanted his grandchildren to be aware that *the current state of rich comfort he had created for us was a rare gift*.

Sometimes at Sunday lunch he recited the words of an old Irish lament from the Famine (he had not wanted his well-fed grandchildren to take their feast of food and their affluence for granted):

"Just give me three grains of corn, Mother," he would recite in what he thought was a shaky child's voice, "Just three grains of corn. It will keep the little life I have until the coming of the morn.

"Just three grains of corn, Mother." Here his voice would rise in a powerful plea, capturing our attention, for he usually was so gentle. "Just *three grains* of corn!"

During the Famine in Ireland the English landowners had huge barns full of corn that they refused to distribute because it would have lowered the price internationally. My grandfather wanted us to remember that just a generation or so ago the Gills might have been starving and begging for just a handful of corn to survive.

Yet my grandfather didn't hate the English or Protestants. He had made his way quickly to the top of the Protestant establishment. Despite being born with nothing, he had worked his way as a scholarship student through Yale and received a medical degree. He went on to study in London and he became a successful surgeon upon his return to Hartford.

Even more surprising for an Irish person at the time—when ads in the local papers still read: "Irish need not apply"—he became a director of three banks in Connecticut. The Connecticut Yankees jealously guarded their money. The banks were their true fortresses. I was told that in those days to even be employed at a bank you had to become a Mason. The Masons had as a core reason for their being a mission to keep Catholics out of power. These tight-fisted Masons loved nothing better than to turn down an Irish Catholic who came in for a loan.

Yet my grandfather had a great gift for math and making money that these stern yet avaricious bankers found impossible to resist. My grandfather became a millionaire at an early age and moved to a commodious mansion on Prospect Avenue, then regarded as the best street in Hartford. Through his brilliance as a surgeon and his talent for making money, he made his way up to the very top of the world in which the old Protestant class still ruled.

My grandfather, who was such a good Catholic that he never charged a priest or a nun for any surgery he performed, also found it wise to send my father to "Protestant schools" without a qualm, because he thought they were the best at that time.

In other words, my grandfather was a good example to me in that he was not an ideologue or a hater in any kind of theoretical sense. He made the best of every reality rather than worrying about past wrongs.

My father attended Noah Webster in his earliest years and then Kingswood Country Day and then went on to Yale. So it was natural that my father's early friends were all Protestants.

If anything my Irish grandfather and father—who liked to

call himself a "Black Irishman" because of his swarthy appearance—were Anglophiles. My grandfather loved to quote the popular Victorian poets—most of whom were English. My father in later life loved to go over to London to appear on a popular BBC quiz show. My father's critical yet rather affectionate view of what he regarded as the comical class system, his rapier wit, and his outrageous attacks on pomposity went over well in England.

So it was hard for me as a person with a proud yet relaxed Irish background myself to understand the level of hate that Jim's father felt for England and Protestants—even to the level of not attending his son's funeral because it was in the "wrong church."

Jim was not about to give in to his father's unreasonable demands. He thought his father was being irrational and Jim was a rational guy.

The great thing about having Jim as a friend to me was his rational, common sense. We would talk for hours late into the night, and Jim would give me a clear vision of what reality was really like. All through our decades together I would love to sit with Jim and discuss the world. Because of my upbringing I was not the most grounded, and when I met with serious clients I would always have to fake my knowledge of how the world really worked. Gradually, my colleagues at JWT would develop a mantra they told clients: "Don't ask Mike about money." Once in a new business meeting I had promised that we would do the advertising for free. That was it for me. From then on they would introduce me with the words: "Good directors are all a little bit crazy. Mike is a *great* creative director."

That simple introduction let the clients know that I was not to be trusted in the real world. Honestly, I am *still* struggling to become more adept at negotiating cash registers and other challenging interactions in the real, retail world I now inhabit.

But Jim knew what was what with money and other key realities. Jim was grounded. I loved him for his sense of reality. And also because he was quick to enjoy what real life could give him. I can see him now with a beer, listening to the opera at full blast.

When we were in high school he had come up one summer and visited me in Norfolk.

"What's that?" Jim had asked, hearing some music.

"*La Traviata*. My mother loves opera; she plays it all the time."

"Great music," Jim said.

He introduced me to Andrés Segovia. When he was in the army, he told me, he would play those gentle guitar notes and found it a great way to end a day.

Jim loved to race his oldest son Benjamin on weekend runs. His second son Michael was with him the last day I saw him in the country. He loved to be surrounded by those he loved.

He often took his whole family, two sons and his daughter Claire, on ski holidays or other adventures. He would so look forward to those times. The Adirondack weekend was typical of his gregarious spirit, he and Barbara with a group of friends in a spot they enjoyed. I could imagine how much fun Jim would have had in that beautiful outdoor setting.

I thought that Barbara, now worrying that Jim had eaten too much or the wrong food and that was what had caused his death, was just trying to make sense of a terrible tragedy. When such a shocking event occurs, I think it is natural that we go back in our mind, searching for any clues. It is human nature to try to explain the unexplainable.

I had a thought at the same time that maybe being fired by Merrill Lynch in the previous year had played some part in Jim's early death. I remembered how hard it had been when I was cast aside. And I was sure that Jim, a very loyal fellow himself, had been hurt by such corporate disloyalty.

Barbara and I were both struggling to find some rational reasons for Jim's sudden death. Maybe it was a combination of everything: being fired, eating too much, having just been diagnosed with a weak heart, and wearing those heavy boots. Plus the sudden shock of the unexpected storm.

"We went for a canoe ride after the picnic. The lake looked so calm and the sun was shining."

Barbara sat down in the kitchen. I sat down with her, holding her shoulder with one hand. She was being so brave, yet this was so hard for her.

"Then a storm came up. One of those wild storms you can get in the Adirondacks. The waves on the lake got huge so quickly. The canoe turned over. Jim was weighted down by those boots, but he insisted we push the boat toward the far shore."

I could see the picture: Jim refusing to give up, pushing with all his might against the waves and the flashes of lightning and the dark clouds. Jim was a strong man still in his prime, and he never quit that kind of physical challenge. Hadn't he carried all of his luggage from the Merritt Parkway when his father had thrown him out of the car?

Just as Jim's father was a fierce hater, Jim was a fierce lover of life and just as strong in his determination. I could imagine Jim refusing to quit. I believe in his heart Jim probably also felt that he must make sure that Barbara got to shore safely. He was that kind of guy. He would take responsibility for others.

"Something went wrong," Barbara continued. "I looked back. Jim wasn't pushing anymore. I let the canoe go and pulled him to shore. But Jim was dead."

How awful that must have been for Barbara. Can you picture being with a vibrant person you love, enjoying life at its height one minute—and the next second seeing him dead beside you, with nothing you could do?

Barbara asked me to sing "Galway Bay" at Jim's funeral. There's a wonderful closing verse in that old Irish song:

> *And if there is a life hereafter.*
> *And somehow I am sure there's bound to be!*
> *Well I hope it's just a bit like that old heaven*
> *In that far land across the Irish sea.*

I think there is a heaven, and I am sure Jim is cheering me on and he is not worried that I still don't quite get reality. But I miss his confident, positive presence so grounded in the key lesson: *Enjoy the current reality rather than imposing old hatreds or ideologies*.

And barely a year or so after Jim died, Barbara was dead as well. She had never much liked yearly physicals, and her doctor had never insisted on colon scans. When she finally had one, she was told that her colon cancer was far advanced. In her last days she insisted on going home to die. She wanted to be with her children.

I went to see her. She was up on the big bed with her kids. I got on the bed as well. We all hugged. Unlike with Jim's sudden death, we had some time to say good-bye. But it was not enough. Her children were bereft. Claire and Michael were just starting college. Benjamin just in college. They needed their parents. Fortunately Barbara's brother is a great uncle, and Jim's siblings also kept in close touch with everyone.

But can you imagine what it must have been like for them to lose their parents just as they were beginning to create their own lives? Jim and Barbara's deaths in such quick succession were a terrible shock to me.

Yet it is sometimes so easy for me to slip back into taking the miraculous gift of life for granted.

When I was working to help the Marines with their advertising, I learned that they never made that mistake: They never take life itself for granted.

One example of the Marines' attitude: When I was in my late thirties and creative director on the Marine Corps account, I decided to run in the marathon they sponsored in Washington, D.C. I had never run anywhere near that distance. It took me over five hours to complete the twenty-plus miles, and I ended up staggering in pain rather than running at the end, but I *did* finish the race, since the Marines had made it clear to me that quitting was not an option.

The next day I was back to work at my office without any obvious strain. Of course, I was thirty-eight at the time—only a kid!

There was a Marine Sergeant Daley in the First World War. His men were confronting German machine guns for the first time in the front lines. They seemed hesitant to charge the storm of killing bullets.

"Come on," he yelled. "Do you want to live *forever*?"

Most of my life I was in a kind of state of denial that I would ever have to die. And, yes, I *did* want to live forever.

When I first started helping the Marine Corps with their recruitment advertising (we developed the line "The Marines are looking for a Few Good Men"), I visited their headquarters and spoke with the man who was in charge of our advertising budget. I couldn't help noticing that the building was right next to Arlington Cemetery.

"Doesn't it make you nervous?" I asked without thinking.

"Nervous? Maybe you guys in advertising don't like to admit it, but we *all* die sometime. We like to have that destination right before us at all times. No Marine takes his life for granted—ever!"

"Yes, *sir*!" I said to General McMillan, realizing I had made a real mistake.

In the next few years of working with the Corps, I came to understand that Marines don't seek death, but they are willing to risk death to protect the rest of us. They *volunteer* for that dangerous duty. So the Marines make sure even the rawest recruit is aware that his or her job is to risk death for America.

"Arlington Cemetery is the best real estate location in Washington," General McMillan told me another time. "I can't wait to occupy some prime space."

The Marines live each day with the constant knowledge that it might be their last. They feel it gives them an extra kick of adrenaline. Having known Marines now for thirty years, I would say I have never met any group that has a greater ability to get the most out of life.

As I have grown older I have grown more comfortable with death. Death is no longer something I fear.

Not that I want to die today. But I feel more at ease with death than I ever did before. I feel like Robert Frost in his description of dying in his poem "Birches":

> *I'd like to get away from earth awhile*
> *And then come back to it and begin over.*
> *May no fate willfully misunderstand me*
> *And half grant what I wish and snatch me away*
> *Not to return. Earth's the right place for love:*
> *I don't know where it's likely to go better.*

Like Robert Frost, I would like to do over many things in my life. I still feel guilty for having hurt my children in my divorce. I still cringe at the idea of how prejudiced I was for much of my life and how little thought I ever gave to others in the sense of seeing them with true compassion. Yet I also agree with Frost that "earth's the right place for love."

I have never felt more in love with my life or with life itself. Yet in a paradoxical way this love of each mortal, evanescent moment has also put me more in touch with the love of God.

When I was a young boy our cook Nana would tell me, "You will be a minister one day."

She believed I had special psychic gifts because I had told her that her father was going to die soon and she should make a special trip down south to see him. Nana didn't make the trip, but her father did die unexpectedly, and from then on she would tell me: "You can see what others can't. You will be a priest or a preacher!"

I was just four or five years old at the time, but I loved Nana and believed her. I felt close to God in those days. Maybe the warm embrace in Nana's generous arms when I came into her kitchen helped to give me that feeling of comfort and faith. But even as a lonely little boy—or maybe especially as a lonely little boy—I felt God's loving presence with me.

Today I feel that presence once again. Not in any heavy way but just in simply having faith that such an immortal love is part of the unfolding of the universe.

My faith and willingness to talk about it has been matched recently in my Starbucks store. There seems to have been a seismic shift recently in America about what one is allowed to discuss. While in earlier years Ray Charles and Otis Redding and Frank Sinatra would be singing songs about pain and life's real tragedies, I never heard Guests discuss such things. Times have changed. Just the other day when I was sweeping, I happened to notice a woman knitting. I had never seen that before in my store.

"What are you doing?" I asked her.

"I'm knitting a prayer shawl," she said.

"What's that?"

"My friend is very sick. With cancer. I knitted her a little cap when she lost her hair. She loved that. So this is a shawl she can have around her shoulders. To comfort her and she can know I love her always."

"My wife died last December," a man said at the next table.

That surprised me. Often Starbucks Guests have long conversations with their friends but it is rare for someone at another table to join in. But the lady seemed to welcome his comment.

"That must have been hard for you," she said.

"It was. I still cry every day."

"Crying is good for you," the shawl lady said.

"Mike." It was Yami calling from the bar. "Could you do me a favor and check the condiment bar? We might need some fresh milk."

I hurried on to do my job. Yami knew me well and realized I could easily spend my shift involved in talking rather than cleaning or helping. But as I fixed up the condiment bar—bringing fresh milk, filling up the five different kinds of sugar, making sure we had plenty of napkins—I thought how surprising it was that two people should be talking with such frankness about the tragedy of life. Yet it was clear their shared communion of grief was a healing moment for both of them.

Yesterday, when I was off work (the joys of a part-time job!), I went in to get my free pound of coffee. One of the great "perks" of working for Starbucks is that every Partner is given a free pound a week. I was waiting in line behind a Guest I recognized. She turned, saw me, and I said: "Where's the little one?"

She was one of the mothers it was such a pleasure to see: so clearly involved in every moment of her daughter's life. Tears sprang into her eyes.

"You haven't heard?"

"I've been away," I said.

My book tours have meant I am not in my store as often as I was before.

"Shannon was sick. Her fever rose to over 105. She was so hot! I went downstairs to see if I could get some medicine for her . . . when I came back . . . she had gone."

"Terrible," I said, "I can't believe it!"

"Neither can I. Peter is going crazy."

Peter is her husband. I had seen the entire family unit in a pizza place down the block. They were laughing and talking with their four-year-old. And now she was dead and gone.

"What happened?"

"No one knows. We had a service two weeks ago. She is buried near here. My family all was here."

Now she was wiping tears away. Not in an embarrassed way, just letting them fall and brushing them away as though it were just a part of her life now.

"We took her to Lawrence Hospital that night—immediately. They didn't even have a pediatrician there. But it was too late, anyway."

She handed me a small photograph.

"Here. You can have this."

I looked at the smiling blond little girl I had gotten to know over the last years.

I found a few tears were clouding my eyes as well. I could not believe that the little girl who'd been such a bundle of cheerful energy was gone. With Shannon's beaming face no longer with us, it was like a space had been taken out of the world. I have kept that picture. I pray for her and her parents every day. I don't know whether my prayers help her, but they help me. By praising them and blessing them I feel some comfort for that terrible and unexpected tragedy.

In fact, even greeting people at the cash register these days I say silent prayers for them. I don't speak them out loud because it might scare them. But I can't resist just saying silently to myself as they come up to my register or walk out the door: "God bless you."

In Ireland they still say "God bless" out loud when you leave a bar or simply say good-bye after conversing on the street. Of course, the word "good-bye" itself is an abbreviation for "God be with you."

Every morning when I do my stretches I say some prayers that seem to just flow out of me. It is not a conscious choice for me to pray. I just keep thanking God for everything. I ask for forgiveness. I pray for strength to be a better person and serve more.

Then I make myself a great cup of coffee.

I feel like God is with me more and more these days. I think that many people—at least in my little store and my little life—are feeling closer to God in these difficult times.

We are no longer in a world where Donald Trump is our only hero. Or firing someone is regarded as a heroic act. Maybe we are realizing that a shared feeling of failure and grief can be redeeming. In these hard times we are becoming more accepting that *death* is a primal fact of *life*.

Living with a sense of peace and acceptance about my mortality has also focused me on making the most of the present. I used to take life for granted and behaved as though I could live forever. Now I am in a continuous state of gratitude and happiness for just being *alive*.

HOW THIS LESSON CAN HELP YOU

Accepting your own approaching death and the inevitable end to your own life, no matter how much you would like to deny or avoid facing that fate, can lead you to be more in touch with the truth and wonder of your journey. Living with the certain fact of your death can add new joy to your life. Remember the valuable lessons of family and friends who have taught you that it is better to love than to hate and that it is important to treat every second as a gift to be grateful for and to enjoy.

Enjoy yourself: It's later than you think!

Late Bloomers . . .
The Last of Life Can Be the Best

"Grow old along with me
The best is yet to be
The last of life
For which the first is made."
   —*Robert Browning, "Rabbi Ben Ezra"*

 I never would have predicted that the last years of my life would be the best. But that is how it feels to me. I have been given in these last years so many happy surprises I would never have imagined.

In a way I feel that God has saved the best for last.

I remember Winston Churchill saying as he became prime minister in his sixth decade: "My entire life has been but a preparation for this hour."

In a simpler and much more humble way I feel that my entire life has led me to this happy ending. Even all the mistakes and missteps I've made have brought me to this moment, where I feel such gratitude for everything I see and do.

And, in some ways, I feel I can do more than ever.

Perhaps there is some mysterious spring of positive feeling that bubbles up in you as you approach the source of the river of life at the end of your years. You know how salmon leap back up the stream they were born in? There is a leaping kind of joy to these last days of my life.

You know how they speak of getting a second wind? I feel an extra burst of energy now as I near my finish line. I don't think this extra dash of life and joy is unique to me. I have seen it in others who went before.

As she moved into her eighties and nineties Brooke Astor seemed to gain an extra zest. She would often be the last to leave the dance floor at parties. My father also went in his later years from a fast walk into a headlong run as he rushed about the city he so loved.

My perceptions these days feel heightened as though I've been given a special clarity. Even the smallest, scruffy weed in a summer field takes on a new beauty as it dances in the late-afternoon sun.

You know how at the end of the day the whole world seems to take on a different yet sometimes even more magical light? Birds start singing their songs with a special force in the long summer twilights. Or perhaps it is just at the close of day we can hear them better.

I think of Leopold Bloom, the hero of Joyce's *Ulysses*, who pauses in his wandering to listen to a song:

> *Just a song at twilight*
> *When the lights are low*
> *And the flickering shadows*
> *Softly come and go*
> *Though the heart be weary*
> *Sad the day, and long*
> *Still to us at twilight*
> *Comes love's old song*
> *Comes love's old sweet song.*

Love blossoms as the birds sing and the shadows fall at the close of day. Hear the chords of enchantment in this hymn to evening written by Sabine Baring-Gould:

> *Now the day is over*
> *Night is drawing nigh*
> *Shadows of the evening*
> *Steal across the sky*

There is no question that in many ways life gets better as we grow in age. We grow more in tune with it and gain wisdom and we are able—given our new perspective—to be more creative with whatever talents we were given at the dawn of our lives.

In our last summers of life not only do we bring a new appreciation to the songs of birds, we also become much more aware and grateful for the talents of everyone else—and the beauty of *every* living thing.

My father wrote a book called *Late Bloomers* that celebrated famous people who achieved their greatest work at an advanced age—such as Grandma Moses, Harry Truman, and Julia Child. The book took its title from the garden term used to describe flowers that bloom late in the season and has come to apply to people as well.

In the introduction my father says of such late bloomers:

... The lateness isn't merely a consequence of the inevitable passage of years and decades. Rather, it has to do with the moment in time at which we discover, whether through an event dictated by forces outside ourselves or by a seemingly spontaneous personal insight, some worthy means of fulfilling ourselves ... what are late bloomers?

They are people who at whatever cost or whatever circumstances have succeeded in finding themselves.

I am happy to join the company of flowers that bloom late in the season.

Sometimes sunsets can be even more beautiful than dawns. Now I love sunsets. The whole world seems to shift a little with a silent sigh. The bright, hot sun of midday is replaced with many more subtle dimensions. As I look out of my attic window, the colors of evening now seem spread with a more generous hand. Today I feel more appreciative of every such scene.

The prophet Elijah speaks of the "still, small voice of God." That voice seems to come to me in the quiet of a soft dusk rather than in the cacophonous midday crush. There is a kind of sacred solitude to many evenings I have now.

You know those silent notes between the sounds of a symphony? I appreciate that quiet stillness more and more.

> *They that wait upon the Lord shall renew their strength*
> *They shall mount up with wings of eagles*
> *They shall run and not be weary*
> *They shall walk and not feel faint.*

This biblical injunction speaks of waiting. And, of course, we also are told: "They also serve who only sit and wait." Americans fear the sedentary life. We are always urged to be "up and doing." Yet sitting in a quiet place can be so refreshing to the spirit. I find silent peace quite nurturing.

I own no television. I know if I had a TV I would become obsessed with all the "talking heads." I would watch it constantly. I would turn it on when I came home just for the company. I know for me the sound of other human voices—if only strangers shouting at each other in a big box—could become addictive.

I can see myself with a remote, flipping through all the channels, looking for stimulation and calling it "education." I have resisted buying a television because it is something I don't think I could resist once it was in front of me. I have found—surprising myself—that silence when I come back to my simple home is best for me. I feel a quiet gratitude and happiness when I let myself experience the solitude.

No more bright lights and late nights in the big city. I like to be in bed by eight o'clock or so, asleep by nine and rising with the first light. Come to think of it, my days now are similar to those we all had before electricity replaced the natural sun and dark night with relentless electric light. Now in my last days I follow the sun, savoring the first dawn and the last rays in the evening.

I have found another happy surprise in growing old: a new-found joy in returning to the older, simpler rhythms of life and light of an earlier age. I have to admit that in many wondrous ways these last years have been the best of my life. And they are still getting better. And better.

So I happily invite you to:

"Come along with me for the best *is* yet to be!"

HOW THIS LESSON CAN HELP YOU

Try a test today: Turn off your television. Look out the window and watch the sun sink. Let that sunset be your visual focus rather than the talking heads on a screen. Listen to birds singing rather than an angry debate. Grant yourself at the close of your day one hour of peace.

Then rise tomorrow with a sure knowledge that you have gained— whatever your age and current circumstances—a sense of how to make the best of every waking moment. And be prepared for these next years to be the best years of your life.

LESSON 14

Less Is More . . .

Lose All Your "Stuff" and Find Freedom

"Born to lose."

—*Ray Charles*

 "I've lost it on the train," I remember my father ex-
claiming one night as he came home just a year or
so after we moved to Bronxville.

"What?" my mother asked him.

"A manuscript. A book I was supposed to review and now it is
gone forever."

"You can check tomorrow in the lost and found," my mother
tried to comfort him. "They will probably have it there."

My father never found the manuscript—he lost many over
the years—but I was intrigued as a young boy by the idea of a
"lost and found."

Yet in a surprising way that is what happened to me: I lost so
much and yet today I feel I have found so much more.

In a paradoxical way maybe we are all born to lose. I was certainly reborn in many ways when I lost my footing on the top
rungs of the American Establishment. I was terrified.

I was terrified and seemed to be losing so fast all I had worked
so hard to gain. First, my job. Then, my big house. I would never

have chosen to lose all my money, my six-figure salary, my big home, and my sense of entitlement. Then, my family through divorce. Finally, my health.

I went from feeling like a winner to feeling like a victim.

I embraced the feeling that my life was a terrible tragedy. I felt that few had lost as much as I. Looking back, I can see now I almost embraced my sense of my horrible destiny. Like the old song I said:

"Nobody knows the trouble I've seen / Nobody knows but Jesus."

In my previous life I loved going to Church on Easter but was made rather uncomfortable by Good Friday and hearing about the martyrdom of Christ. Why couldn't Jesus—of all people—have been spared such pain?

He even says: "Father, Father why have Thou forsaken me?"

The fact that Jesus was crucified was something I didn't exactly ignore, but it was an aspect of the story I had trouble incorporating into my life.

I loved going into a church on Madison Avenue and hearing: "We stand in the light of the resurrection."

In other words we don't have to suffer because Jesus has already suffered enough for our sins. Alas, this rosy view of life has no basis in any true religious teaching. While Jesus might have suffered to redeem us, He cannot protect us from our own failings.

I don't claim that I experienced any of the loss willingly. I am no St. Francis. His father was a wealthy merchant. In his youth, so the histories say, St. Francis was happy to dress up and play the gallant knight. He was apparently quite a ladies' man and not at all averse to showing off by fighting battles he thought he could easily win. But then he suddenly threw off all such mortal delights. He wore barely any clothes and became what was once called "a fool for God."

Yet St. Francis's "foolishness" was actually a deeper wisdom. As the Bible says: "Lay not your treasure upon earth where moss and rust doth corrupt."

I learned the hard way that there is no security in owning Wall Street securities or in being loyal to a "company" rather than a faith.

Buddha was said to have left his princely home to find his sense of peace. I am no Buddha. I would never have left the princely income afforded by my job or my big home unless I had been forced to.

Yet I feel it was a kind of divine grace that stepped in and gave me a chance to lose my materialistic life so that I could find a happier and more fulfilling way to live. I hasten to add that I don't regard myself as a saint or as any better than anyone still struggling to find their way. I just feel fortunate that I was given the chance to see that immortal truth: Losing so much in life can give you a much better life.

Let me be clear: This perception is not unique to me. It has been voiced and lived throughout the ages by every kind of teacher in every kind of civilization. In fact, I now see how stupid I was to regard my losses as particularly tragic and to see myself as the plaything of unkind fates rather than the recipient of final truths.

And I was equally stupid to think that my experience of material loss leading to a happier life is an exceptional occurrence. Billy, one of my favorite Guests, always has a smile and a positive energy to share.

"Why are you so happy?" I asked him one day.

"Because I—like you—once lived a big life and lost it. I was getting paid thousands of dollars a day. I lost it to drugs and alcohol. But now I found a job as a consultant for others who have an addiction. In my new job I am much happier than I ever was running around as a kind of playboy of the Western world. I spent millions theoretically having a good time"—Bill smiled—"but after I lost my money I found that it's a lot more rewarding to help others—as best I can—than it is trying to spend big bucks to get happiness."

I really enjoyed many of my material possessions and my sense of privileged status. Yet I cannot deny that today I am grateful for what I've lost because of the new kind of happiness I have found.

I was forced to become more humble and live in the real world in which nobody cared where I went to school or who my parents were. And I came face to face every day with the fact that I was fortunate just to be alive and have a chance to interact with people of every background and talent.

The loss of material possessions can often result in a new kind of happiness of spirit. Only through losing all of my measures of material and external success was I able to discover this truth.

When Mies van der Rohe said "less is more," he was speaking of architecture, but his point is also true of life.

We all come into this life without any luggage. But by the time I was in my fifties I was like those travelers you see struggling frantically through an airport, burdened with lots of extra bags of heavy stuff they have picked up on their trip, stumbling to maintain their balance and not drop anything as they race to catch a plane.

I spent most of my life working so hard to accumulate material possessions. I did not realize that with every eager purchase, I was also adding to the weight of the world I carried on my shoulders.

"Stuff" has a peculiar way of occupying not only your mind but also your heart and even soul. Usually you can't stop thinking about your stuff when you look forward to getting it and then fear losing it. Often you fall so in love with your stuff that you can't even bear to throw out a "chotchka" that you bought years ago on some trip that you can barely remember.

Finally you give up your soul and make deals with devils to keep a job you hate so you can keep all the stuff you bought. The concern for keeping stuff adds a constant worry to your life. It is like a low-grade fever: You are never free from the fear of losing the stuff you worked so hard to acquire.

I remember my first boss at J. Walter Thompson, Dwight Davis, gave me a big piece of advice with my first raise: "Congratulations, Mike," he said, "but I have to warn you: The richer you get, the more you worry about being poor."

Dwight spoke the truth: The more money I had, the more I spent and the more I lived in an anxious mood of always trying to make more.

I have known billionaires who wake up each morning with a kind of deep-seated paranoia: They are afraid their good fortune cannot last. There is no security in money: only greater fear that somehow it could all disappear someday.

The more money you have, the more you have to lose, and so the sick fear grows.

Frank Capra made a wonderful movie during the Great Depression titled *You Can't Take It with You*. Yet so many spend their lives building up fortunes as though such an effort could assure some hope of immortality.

Money is the easiest drug in a material culture to get hooked on. A big house is also irresistible. But once you have a huge house you have to make sure you have a big job to pay the mortgage. Once you have a huge house and a big job you not only fear their loss, you lie awake at night wondering whether you can survive without all the goodies you have gained.

Make a list of the things you have sacrificed so much of your time and life force to acquire. Then list the things you actually *need to survive*. The bare necessities. You will discover that you don't need most of the things you have, and you can live easily (and oftentimes are even better off) without those possessions.

As humans, we need food on the table and a roof over our heads. But equally, we need family and love. We need to appreciate the world we live in and respect those around us. We don't need fancy clothes, or matching silverware, or the fastest car, or the most up-to-date anything. There is a natural and sadly inevitable tendency to become *possessed by our possessions*.

I have discovered the only sure way to avoid that fate: Don't buy more stuff! And get rid of all the stuff you can.

As we eagerly fill our lives full to overflowing, I have come to understand a basic fact: *Any* fool can complicate their lives.

It takes a genius to simplify.

The best way to simplify: Free yourself from stuff!

While many of our possessions may bring us temporary comfort, they inevitably bring burdens as well—the burden of paying for them, of maintaining them, of them getting in the way of our thoughts and our time.

Stuff clogs our lives like cholesterol can clog our arteries. Stuff can weigh us down emotionally and mentally in ways we don't even recognize. I used to find myself straining through my days, striving so hard without really understanding that a large part of my effort was simply carrying stuff I didn't really need.

Today as I climb the stairs to my little attic apartment I look forward to what we used to call in advertising "white space." When I open the door to my apartment I see white walls and white plastic picnic furniture. There's a lot of welcome white space.

A reporter came to interview me and see the way I lived. First we walked up to the home where I had grown up: a twenty-five-room mansion built in an imposing style that seemed fit for a king. Then we came back to my little apartment so lacking in expensive furniture or any other stuff.

"I have to say something," the reporter told me with a frown, "but not as a reporter. This is not about my newspaper story—this is about the way you *live*."

"Okay," I said, ready for some profound observation about my life.

"You have to get a couch!" she announced.

No, I don't. No couch. My life is a lesson that the loss of stuff can bring a new sense of liberty. I feel a whole new sense of freedom from the fear of losing stuff.

I also feel free of the literal and proverbial weight of carrying all such stuff. I have found how much fun it can be to travel through life without carrying a lot of luggage!

Somehow in recent years we have let the American Dream become defined as an aspiration for possessions. Life, liberty, and the pursuit of happiness do not mean the greedy desire for more stuff.

Tonight my sleep is not weighed down by my fear of losing my possessions.

When I wake I walk without the burden of all that stuff.

HOW THIS LESSON CAN HELP YOU

When loss happens to you, be prepared to find something new. There is an essential truth to all teachings for thousands of years: Loss of material possessions can often result in new kind of happiness of the spirit.

Look upon physical stuff as something to get rid of—not as something to keep. Understand that our American Declaration of Independence, when it described the pursuit of happiness, did not mean the acquisition of stuff. Liberty and independence can be granted to you at this minute by finding yourself a way to live without so much stuff.

LESSON 15

Love . . . The Ride and
Let Your Light Shine

"This little light of mine
I'm gonna let it shine."
  —*Spiritual Song*

After I gave a talk at a bookstore in Colorado last month a person waved her hand, eager to ask a question.

I nodded at her. She bounced up out of her seat, obviously a very athletic person and full of barely contained energy.

"Have you ever gone white-water rafting?" she asked.

"No," I stammered, having never been asked that question before.

The rest of the audience also turned surprised looks at her. It was not a typical question.

"Your book reminds me of white-water rafting," she said. "You start out in a placid stream . . . then you hit rapids. Sometimes you lose control and just have to go with it, sometimes you turn over. It almost seemed to me you felt like you were drowning. Then you struggle and learn to really swim with the current. At the end there's a kind of tranquil stream where you are happier than ever."

"That does sound like my story," I said, and everyone laughed because her metaphor did indeed seem to capture the flow of my story in a new way. The woman had a valuable point to make. I had been born in a river in full flood of good fortune. When the current changed and I hit real rapids, I didn't know what to do.

Today I understand that life is full of peaceful moments when everything seems to be going well, yet it can just as quickly take a terrible turn, where you find yourself upended over a waterfall. The sadness, shock, surprise, and joy of life are inextricably intermixed in a way that is impossible to separate. Misadventures, in other words, are an essential part of the adventure of life—you simply can't have one without the other.

Life is full of uncertainty—a fact that is both its challenge and its excitement. Understanding and accepting this basic life truth helps turn the tumultuous ride on the rushing river of life from one full of dread into one full of joy and awe. Take comfort in knowing that the ride will be amazing.

It *is* one heck of a ride.

But that is life. You can't go through life without experiencing great moments of peace and furious times when everything seems like it is going wrong and you could easily wipe out. At the end of most white-water rafting experiences you come out again onto a broad, sunlit expanse of water waiting to welcome you. Or so I have heard and like to believe!

I know for certain: You can't hide on the shore in life. We are all on the river. The only choice we have is whether we can learn to love the ride or spend our time screaming at the unkindness of our fate.

There is no perfect white-water rafting experience—all are full of unexpected moments of excitement and fear. And there is no perfect life. Or even a perfect person. We were created imperfect and I think part of the miracle of our lives is that we get to participate in trying to make ourselves a bit better. God could have created us perfect. Instead we have a chance to play a major role in the creation of our lives.

Even people we'd consider perfect or "lucky" are also struggling to find happiness. My experience is that while the rich and famous might look perfect or "lucky" from a distance, when you come close their lives are at least as full of pain and agony and personal struggles as any of the rest of us. There is no missing the rapids or being tossed over the waterfall in *any* life.

I have given up trying to cling to any particular stones along the shore or build up a fortress to protect me from the flow. A decade ago I huddled with fear on the shore. Now I leap with a kind of joyous faith, far out to the very middle of the current. My heart rises as the river rises.

I don't expect to avoid the rapids anymore. But I know that deep inside I will be saying, even when I am upended, what an amazing ride!

The key to happiness is learning to love the ride that is your own unique life and learning to appreciate that each person has a unique story to tell.

As I have been meeting many thousands of people in all different cities across America in the last two years, I am always struck by how many wonderful stories there are inside each person I meet.

Everyone's story is entirely unique to them. My hope is that everyone will let his or her own unique voice be heard. Yet many are hesitant to speak from their heart and reveal their own true identity.

Many readers have told me how grateful they are that I had the courage to tell my story. It was not easy for me.

Gillian MacKenzie, who is my agent and creative catalyst, told me when we shared our first latte: "I will help you get your story published but I don't want to do a book just about Starbucks. I want a book about you and your surprising life. But *only* if you tell the *truth*."

Since I am a former advertising guy, it was not exactly natural for me to tell the truth. But once I began down the road of trying to tell an honest story, I found I felt relieved. I had many feelings bottled up inside of me that I had never really shared—even with myself. When I was fired I pretended in front of family and friends that it was all okay. Even when I first began at Starbucks I tried to hide from my Partners how terrified I was that I might fail at this new opportunity.

In the question-and-answer period after I have given a talk I am almost always asked: "How did you write your book?"

Telling the truth in my story was helped by the fact that I had kept a journal. When I was going through my hard times my daughter Annie suggested I write down just a few sentences of what I was feeling before I went to bed each night.

After about a year of working at Starbucks I reread the journal. I read my descriptions of how despairing and depressed and fearful I was at the beginning, and then, just a year later, how happy I had become. I thought that this story of my transformation and the happy ending to my hard times would be worth telling.

And I *have* heard that my story has been helpful to many who have been fired, or have lost their homes, or even are diagnosed with a serious disease and have no health insurance. All the people in America and around the world have challenges that most books don't even talk about.

My story does face these facts and I deliver the good news that there is life—even a better life—after losing the external measures of success. I can feel from people I talk with that they are reassured and even inspired by my surprising story of the joys of finding my new, simpler life.

Then I turn to the audience and ask them for their stories—and there are always some wonderful ones to hear. I tell everyone: "Tell your story. You can be confident your story will be unlike any told before."

Each of us has a unique and powerful story to tell that might help others navigate their lives. Your story does not have to be in any way too dramatic. Sometimes in our culture of violence and graphic sexual imagery some potential writers feel that they must deal with life in some kind of shocking way to get noticed.

Great stories can be about very simple and beautiful lives. One of the great gifts of my life is people who recommend books to me with stories I otherwise might have missed.

Norman Holmes Pearson, a professor of mine at college who also became a friend, told me I should read a book called *The Country of the Pointed Firs*. It was written by a woman named Sarah Orne Jewett.

At this time in my life I was more in love with Herman Melville and his book *Moby Dick*—such a dramatic story of danger and adventure.

I had never heard of such a book or the woman who wrote it. It definitely didn't sound like my cup of tea. But because I could never resist a book, I found a copy and began to read. She had me from the first page.

Sarah Orne Jewett's tone of passionate love for the old fishing villages along the coast of Maine gripped me with a surprising power. In her clear prose that seemed to sparkle like the strong Maine sunlight she developed a story that was fresh even to my young eyes. The old fishermen and women of those villages became alive with a powerful interest. I couldn't put her book down until I had finished it.

Jewett's fishing captains were so different than Melville's. Her captains seemed at peace with the sea and the natural world they inhabited, while Melville's Captain Ahab fought with a passionate obsession against his fate.

Two people told such different stories about what it was like to spend your life at sea. Even the sea itself can be described in as many ways as there are writers.

Virginia Woolf catches the sound and rhythm of the waves in her book of that name:

"The wave paused, and then drew out again, sighing like a sleeper whose breath comes and goes unconsciously."

F. Scott Fitzgerald ends *The Great Gatsby* with his famous siren song:

"So we beat on, boats against the current, borne back ceaselessly into the past."

I am sure Sarah Orne Jewett and Herman Melville and Virginia Woolf and F. Scott Fitzgerald would have found something to appreciate in the others' very singular and original views of the world. I am also certain they would find that each one of them saw the sea in totally different ways.

For no two authors—no two people—see and describe their experiences in exactly the same way. We all have our *own* stories to tell. We are all made to be original. We are, in that sense, original artists creating our own lives.

Each writer and every poet not only has a unique story to tell but also tells it in a unique way. It is by sharing one another's original sights and senses and stories and communicating the truth about our lives that we can build a civilization we can all enjoy in the future.

I know now that no two lives are alike. Every parent knows that each child is a gift with a unique personality and talents that shine with their own special light.

The impulse to tell our story in some unique way is deep in

our nature. Years ago I went to visit the Lascaux Caves in France. They are full of mystery—but there is no mystery about why our earliest ancestors thousands of years ago filled the walls of these caves with paintings. The walls of these caves are alive with artistic versions of the hunt or the death of a hunter. Such art should not surprise us. We are all created with a desire to celebrate the world around us with drawings and other artistic visions, captured in every medium possible.

Every child born has the ability to relate to the world in their own artistic way. Young children naturally sing and draw and dance. Aren't refrigerators in America at this moment festooned with the artistic works of potential young geniuses? And there *is* a kind of genius in these young artistic efforts. For all great art springs from the same essential source as a desire to share one's own vision with the world. The greatest artists are able to draw for their whole lives on this elemental spring of creation—continuing to display, like Picasso in his productive nineties, a childlike gift for expressing themselves in a way that helps us to see the world fresh each day.

I have several paintings and drawings by my children on my walls. Each child draws and sings and tells stories not out of some desire to be rich or famous—but out of a deeper, more wonderful and profound instinct to give *meaning to life. And every child wants their artistic efforts to be recognized and appreciated.*

Recently I was asked to give a talk at Google. I told them that they were one of the latest expressions of the passionate human need to find new and ever more creative ways to communicate. From the first stone etchings to the printing press and now the Internet our human history is one long saga of the desire to *communicate* in the best possible way and as frequently as possible.

Afterward my Google hosts took me toward the "cafeteria." Some "cafeteria"! Chefs waited to give me a choice of a half dozen salads, three kinds of fish and two kinds of meat. But I was even more impressed by what I saw on the way to the culinary treat. We passed the usual—for Silicon Valley—corporate campus amenities such as sand volleyball courts and swimming facilities. We also passed by rather solid looking containers.

"What are those for?" I asked. They seemed out of place on the lovely campus in their awkward, rather old-fashioned, bulky presence—so far from the elegant, hip Google style.

"You just drop dirty your clothes in there," Marcia told me, gesturing at a container as we went by, "and you get them back in twenty-four hours, cleaned and pressed."

Now I was *really* impressed! Clean laundry was a perk I could really relate to. Then I remembered: Well, in addition to a free pound of coffee every week, Starbucks also cleans my green apron after every shift. Not too shabby. Yet even more impressive than the free laundry offered by Google was the dramatic visual demonstration of *communication* I passed by next. It was a huge globe vibrating with millions of pinpoints of light. Our planet Earth was lit up in real time by every Google hit. Millions and millions of tiny lights going off simultaneously in nanoseconds.

What more powerful demonstration of our desire to connect and *communicate with one another—to share our light?* All those millions of intense lights constantly flashing with an almost manic intensity are a vibrant, visual symbol of our capacity and love for communicating.

Robert Frost once said: "Only when the need and love are one / Is the deed ever really done / For heaven's and the future's sake." Communicating is our greatest *need* and greatest *love* and we have never ceased in our desire to find new ways to make that magic happen.

That is why many ancient civilizations have used art and stories to communicate and to add meaning and even beauty to their

lives. In tribal civilizations dancers would gather around a campfire wearing carefully crafted masks of monsters or of the animals
they needed to survive. Others would sing songs of battles done
or battles yet to come.

The Mayan writings have finally been translated and are full
of detailed and compelling action stories that feature their share
of mighty heroes. The Inca were another civilization that spoke
in stone carvings of a great empire's dramatic rise. The Egyptian
tombs tell of a people devoted to creating rich murals that celebrated various aspects of their lives. The simplest carvings recovered from the oldest sites in the ancient world have scratchings
that seem to convey some clear effort to make more sense of the
world through communicating with one another.

The impulse to make up stories and to make sense of things
was also linked to a desire to express our deepest senses—from
the hunger for food to the hunger for love.

One of my favorite love poems is the "Song of Solomon":

> *My beloved spake, and said unto me, Rise up, my love, my*
> *   fair one, and come away.*
> *For, lo, the winter is past, the rain is over and gone;*
> *The flowers appear on the earth; the time of the singing of*
> *   birds is come, and the voice of the turtle is heard in our*
> *   land;*
> *The fig tree putteth forth her green figs, and the vines with*
> *   the tender grape give a good smell. Arise, my love, my*
> *   fair one, and come away.*

We are made to dance and made to sing together. We are created to celebrate and share our love and our love for life.

To do so we should let go of the past, or the shyness we sometimes learn as adults when we've lost our so-called childish artis-

tic confidence. Even as adults, even growing old, we should find ways to let our own light shine out with the knowledge that this is what we were created to do.

Near the end of his life the Irish poet William Butler Yeats said:

> *When such as I cast out remorse*
> *So great a sweetness flows into the breast*
> We must laugh and we must sing,
> We are blest by everything,
> *Everything we look upon is blest.*

Dancing and singing is our natural birthright. These are blessings to be enjoyed. We should embrace our right to share our own unique stories through singing or dancing or drawing or writing—each and every day. We should never be too shy about letting our light shine.

And we should not expect that our vision will be like that of anyone else's.

I even discovered that there are three adult versions of me out there, but that we are all very different. I went back to Ireland to look for my roots, to a tiny town called Drumsna on the banks of the Shannon. The Gills had emigrated from a river in Ireland to the Connecticut River. I drove through Drumsna a couple of times before I could find it. The town is just a single garage and a church, a small row of houses and, of course, a pub.

I visited the pub. It was early afternoon.

"Sure, no one will be in at this hour," the barman assured me, "but come back later."

I told him I was searching for any members of the family.

"And what be your name?"

"Michael Gill."

"Oh, sure we are thick on the ground here with Gills. Why, you can meet three Michael Gills this very evening if you have the patience to wait a bit."

I waited happily. I went for a long walk along the beautiful Shannon River and came back to the pub later that evening. I did, indeed, meet the "three Michael Gills."

One was a university student. One was a farmer. One was an old man who told me: "I'll sing you 'Danny Boy' in Gaelic for five pounds." I didn't take him up on his offer.

In fact the old Michael Gill rather frightened me. Is that the way I might end up . . . promising to sing some distant relative a song . . . for cash? But the farmer, middle-aged, with calloused hands, still wearing his Wellington boots, was a better version of my name. And the university student, energetically brushing hair out of his eyes and delighted to meet a relative from America, was my favorite.

I did not spend that night in Drumsna. There is no hotel, and although I was invited to stay at his farm by the middle-aged Michael Gill, I felt I'd had enough of life's genetic and namesake mystery. We probably did share some of the same genes in addition to our names. But look at how different we all turned out to be!

Some of it was nature versus nurture. My namesakes were formed in Ireland and I in America. Yet there was no disguising how different they were from me and each from the other. There was no mold for Michael Gill any more than there is a duplicate for any one of us. Just as when you look at snowflakes under a microscope and you can see that each one has its own special design, so we are all created to be original.

There's a phrase you hear often at funerals: "They broke the mold" when they made so and so. My feeling now is that it is not so much that a mold was broken, but that there *is no mold for anything*. Creation is a *creative* act that is continually bringing something wholly new and fresh to life. If no two snowflakes are alike, then why should it be so surprising that each of us has our own special life and light to share?

One of the saddest stories in the Bible is of the man who buried his talents. He wanted to keep them safe. He lost them from lack of use. We are each given true talents at birth. God creates each of us with our own special gifts. That is why at the end of my talks I always encourage everyone to: Tell your story. Let your light shine.

Then our whole world will be a better and brighter place.

HOW THIS LESSON CAN HELP YOU

You can learn to enjoy life as an adventure that is always fresh and new if you let yourself be taken where the river wants to go. Know that you are special; you have your own original story to tell, for the course of the river is always changing, and everyone leads a very different life.

If you are reading this book you might like to write. Start keeping a journal. Every night before you go to sleep write a sentence or two about your day or anything that occurs to you. After a few months take a look back at those pages. Then you might decide you have a story worth sharing with others.

Whatever talent you have, whatever you like to do that truly defines you, don't wait to do it! Write or speak or dance or sing—communicate in whatever medium you choose, and as often as you like, and share your unique light!

ONE CONCLUDING, HOPEFUL WISH

When my bubble of privilege burst, I was terrified.

But that breaking of my bubble turned out to be the best thing that ever happened to me.

It freed me to be me.

With the help of many others I made my own way out into a new world that was so much more marvelous than any I had experienced in my protected bubble.

This new world I discovered is an uplifting universe full of love and the deep understanding of the wondrous miracle of life itself.

Today I feel a constant sense of joy and gratitude. When my bubble burst, I was forced to create a new way to live that has brought me a whole new dimension of happiness. I can truly say that today I am happier than ever with my life.

I hope that my hard-won life lessons will also help you to move forward and discover a new way to create a deeper level of happiness in your life.

When I sign my book for someone after sharing my story, I always inscribe my greatest wish for them. It is also my heartfelt wish for you:

"Here's to creating a life you love!"

ACKNOWLEDGMENTS

There is one, single person who is most responsible for the idea of this book. Bill Shinker told me: "I like to publish books that help people." He thought publishing a book that could help people in a very immediate way in these challenging times would be an effort well worth making. I also wish to thank Bill's mother for creating such an extraordinary son. Bill is a great publisher but has also become an invaluable friend—the kind you know is fighting for you even harder than you might fight for yourself.

Bill chose Jessica Sindler to become my editor, and I am so grateful to Jessica's rare talent for adding clarity and a positive narrative flow to my work. Jessica has a perfect touch and is a pleasure work with.

Gillian MacKenzie, my agent and friend, remains my creative catalyst. Gillian is one of those invaluable spirits who bring a spark and a sense of drama to the craft of storytelling.

My valued agent in Hollywood is the intelligent and energetic Shari Smile of Creative Artists Agency. Shari told me that Tom Hanks, Gus Van Sant, and John Orloff are working hard to bring my story to the screen. I am so happy to be with what I believe is "the A team."

Speaking of teams, Lisa Johnson has built a wonderful publicity team that does so much to spread the word. Beth Parker, for example, is a real star at making sure every appearance in every medium goes so well. Beth is such a stimulating person that you feel like you've had a great cup of coffee after talking with her. Adenike Olanrewaju is another excellent publicity person whose calm presence is able to make good things happen.

I appreciate all the people at Gotham/Penguin who have made extra efforts on my behalf.

My thanks for my children are beyond any words. They have been so supportive and loving and understanding. I feel blessed to have such an uplifting support group. I should also give a special shout out to Breda and Elsie, and to all my siblings, nephews, nieces, and cousins—many of whom I have been able to connect with during the last year. I have discovered that it is fun to be part of a tribe that seems to exist in virtually every place in the world.

I also have a special thanks to my accountant with a big heart. Yes, I know that sounds unlikely. But Lawrence Best stood by me in my most difficult times. Larry accepted Starbucks cards for his kids in payment when I had little else to offer. Larry and his wife Anne never gave up on me. Although, when my book became a bestseller and there was news of a film, Larry called to me to advise: "Don't give up your day job!" Larry has helped me become more in tune with the mystery of money.

Speaking of money, despite my continuing difficulties in understanding how to deal with financial reality, I have had the great good fortune of meeting Margaret Cummings–Eachron, who works so hard at the IRS office in New York City. Despite being so busy, Margaret took the time to treat me with courtesy and respect. With her kind help I was able to bring my taxes up to date.

They say death and taxes cannot be avoided, but I would like to take this moment to thank those great doctors who have helped postpone my exit and have actually helped make my current life healthier and happier, including the doctors Lawrence Cohn, Patrick Kelly, Tom Roland, Barstow, and Billo.

Great friends whom I love and who have stayed loyally by my side are Laton and Nancy McCartney, Helen Tucker, Phyllis Samitz Cohen, Kent Berwick, Janet Ross, Kate Wenner, Lucy Danziger, Elena Kroulas, Philip Koutsis, Rita and Alan Steinkamp, Benjamin and Barbara Zucker, Don and Erika Robertson, Joe and Allison Fox, Bill and Barbara Nordhaus, Larry Gwin, Peter and Anne Becket, Jonathan Rose and his family, Dick Moser, Steve Jones, Hank Hewitt, Lee Marsh, Patrick Rulon-Miller, Bill and Lucy Hamilton, Molly and Dave Boren, Tim O'Connell, Jesse Clay, Charlie and Betty Frank, Harry Davison, Coit Liles, Star and Michele Childs, John Wilbur, Jim and Susan Brewster, Stuart and Christopher and Betsy Little, Caroline and Dyck Andrus, Hank Higdon, Dave Mawicke, Susan and Curtis Rand, Aaron and Sasha Childs, Matthew Brennan, Conor McCarthy, Sheila Paterson, Dilys Evans, Robo, Paul Gorman, Robert Grossman, Mike and Tina Cibelli, the Miller family, the Barnard family, including cousins Eaton and Henry Barnard, Santiago Lyon, John Shaw, Tony Thompson, Michael Helme de Havenon, Van Vechten Burger, Freddie Butler, Edward Nusbaum, Ted Wagner, and Jody and Tommy Gill.

Every day I have much to thank my Partners and Guests for, and I wish to pay them the respect of listing their first names (we focus on first names at Starbucks):

Howard

Zeta

Martin

Tasha

Mike

Matt

Anne

Aya

Tamar

Jim

Larry

Magdalena

George

Margaret Ann

Yamileth

Donte

Meghan

Chloe

Jordan

Jonathan

Kamilah

Rachel

Aimee

Mary Louise

Janie

Bob

Lou

Kate

Georgia

Sarah

Billy

Dan

Maldon

Maria

Amy

Steve

Martin

Debbie

Elizabeth

Vinnie

Blaise

Donald

Lisa

Christopher

Nancy

Alma

Carmela

Nick

Molly

Edwin

Gloria

Malcom

Paula

And everyone yet to come!